CW01085179

WINGS WITHOUT WEAPONS

First published in 2008 by

WOODFIELD PUBLISHING LTD
Bognor Regis ~ West Sussex ~ England ~ PO21 5EL
www.woodfieldpublishing.com

© Humphrey Wynn, 2008

All rights reserved.
No part of this publication may be reproduced
or transmitted in any form or by any means,
electronic or mechanical, nor may it be stored
in any information storage and retrieval system,
without prior permission from the publisher.

The right of Humphrey Wynn
to be identified as Author of this work
has been asserted in accordance with
the Copyright, Designs and Patents Act 1988

ISBN 1-84683-054-0

WINGS WITHOUT WEAPONS

A Wartime Pilot's Story

Humphrey Wynn

Woodfield

Woodfield Publishing Ltd

Woodfield House ~ Babsham Lane ~ Bognor Regis ~ West Sussex ~ PO21 5EL
telephone 01243 821234 ~ **e-mail** enquiries@woodfieldpublishing.com

Interesting and informative books on a variety of subjects

For full details of all our published titles, visit our website at
www.woodfieldpublishing.com

Oh, blessed quality of books, that makes them a refuge from living! For in a book everything can be made to fit in, all tedium can be skipped over, and the intense moments can be made timeless and eternal ....

Hilaire Belloc
The Path to Rome

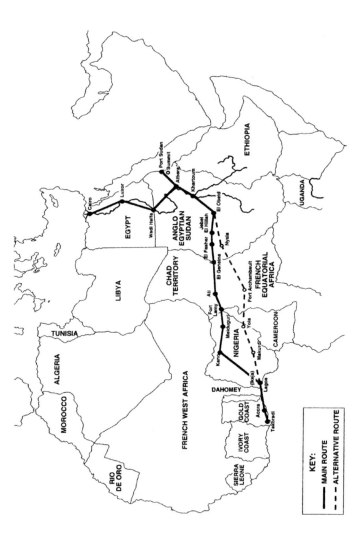

The West African Reinforcement Route (reproduced from the author's *Forged in War ~ A History of Royal Air Force Transport Command 1943-1967*, by permission of the publishers, Her Majesty's Stationery Office 1996)

~ CONTENTS ~

Prologue

In a poem by Hilaire Belloc called *Dedicatory Ode* there are some moving lines,

> *From quiet homes and first beginnings,*
> *Out to the undiscovered ends...*

which exactly describe the circumstances of hundreds of young men who joined the RAF in the Second World War.

As one of them, from a stable family in a suburban house and with only the glimmerings of character, I can vouch for the accuracy of these lines. The ends were yet to be discovered, in the war years, when so many of my contemporaries were caught and died in horrific situations. I was lucky to survive, and dedicate this account of my experiences to their memories.

In September 1939 I was about to begin my second year at Manchester University and went across Oxford Road to the Recruiting Office to volunteer for the RAF.

Nothing happened then until January 1940, when I was called to RAF Cardington in Bedfordshire (site of the hangar for the ill-fated airship R101) to be attested.

This apparently simple ceremony had two complications for me. When asked by a Group Captain at an aircrew selection board a question involving trigonometry, I gave an incorrect answer and he told me my maths were not good enough; I would have to be an air gunner. This depressed me, for I had had visions of becoming a fighter pilot on Hurricanes. The other demoralising factor was the weather, which changed dramatically, and I trudged home to West Didsbury in the early hours of the following morning in deep snow.

The maths business, however, I could do something about – and did; for I was determined to be a pilot. I took special maths tuition and applied for another interview, which I had again at Cardington – when I was called up into the RAF in July 1940, having had a deferment – during which I could wear my small silver lapel badge with RAFVR on it – in order to take my University exams in June. This time my interview was successful; but because of the bottleneck in pilot training, it was to be a long time before I got started. I was posted from Cardington to Morecambe, as an ACH (GD) (Aircrafthand – General Duties), the lowest form of animal life in the RAF. This was a salutary, humbling, experience; I remember cleaning the floors and toilets in the RAF dental surgery. But boy, were we fit! The weather was glorious and we were given drill and PT on the promenade. I remember with special affection the corporals who commanded our Flights (the RAF always maintained aeronautical nomenclature) and the landladies who ran the boarding houses which had been commandeered and in which we were billeted.

During all this time the Battle of Britain was raging in the south of England (though at the time we probably didn't realise its epic significance) and Bomber Command was countering the possibility of a German invasion with its brave but vulnerable Hampden, Whitley and Wellington crews.

At last I got the first inkling of pilot training – a posting to the Aircrew Receiving Centre at Babbacombe in Devon, a beautiful county with its red earth, the green of the fields and the blue of the sea – a sort of autumnal paradise, shattered every now and then by Luftwaffe Ju 88s on hit-and-run raids from their bases in Occupied France.

The Receiving Wing sorted out u/t (under training) aircrew, distinguished by white flashes in their forage caps, for posting to Initial Training Wings – at Torquay, Paignton and Newquay: at these ITWs – I went to Paignton – we were marched everywhere, given more drill and PT and classes in Air Force Law, meteorology, airmanship and navigation, to fit us for the next step – flying at Elementary Flying Training Schools. I was posted to No 16 EFTS at Burnaston, Derby, which had Miles Magister two-seat trainers – which, unlike its contemporary DH82A biplane Tiger Moth, had a tail wheel and brakes.

We were accommodated in Denstone College, and I had a red Ever Ready portable radio; I remember my favourite listening was Vera Lynn singing 'Room Five Hundred and Four'. I can't have been very good at flying, because it took me just over ten hours to go solo; but my instructor, Flying Officer Ron Chalmers, was very patient with me and I've always been grateful to him. I met him again in post-war years when he was with Blackburn Aircraft, as a retired Wing Commander.

From EFTS there were two streams of training – on to single-engined or twin-engined aircraft. I was posted to No. 12 SFTS (Service Flying Training School), at Grantham, which had one Flight of Avro Ansons (ex-operational aircraft) and another of Airspeed Oxfords. I went to the Anson Flight, and qualified for my flying badge (Wings) at the end of May 1941. By then I had done 147 hours 15 minutes flying.

The next step, normally, before becoming an operational pilot was to go to an OTU (Operational Training Unit): I fully expected to go to one with Blenheims or Wellingtons. Instead I was posted, as one of a course of about 15 pilots, to the Service Ferry Squadron at Kemble in Gloucestershire.

The reason for this (although we didn't know it at the time – we'd been in the RAF long enough to know that we just had to do what we were told) was that pilots were needed to fly aircraft up the West African Reinforcement Route from Takoradi to Cairo, to supply the squadrons in the Middle East Air Force, then about to face its greatest challenges in the Western Desert and the Mediterranean.

At Kemble we did rapid conversions on to types we would be likely to fly "up the route": Hurricane, Tomahawk and Maryland (which had French instrumentation because they were destined for France before the German invasion), and the relevant trainer types to help in our conversions – Oxfords and Miles Masters. I think the only reason we didn't kill ourselves on such an assortment of types was that we were innocents, with very little flying experience.

While we were doing our flying at Kemble, those of us who were sergeant pilots were accommodated in Steinbrook House, about two miles from Chippenham, so could walk back after the dances in the Corn Exchange. The local girls couldn't get enough of these young pilots – the RAF was high in national esteem – and when the time came to move on, first to the transit camp at Wilmslow and then by train to Liverpool to board our troopship, there were not a few broken hearts. One of our chaps, Bob Smart, got engaged to "Midge" Hichisson. More of that anon.

My most poignant memory, apart from a last visit to my parents and my sister Margaret, was when we were lined up on the platform at Wilmslow Station waiting for our train; for on the opposite platform were Tom Wagner, father of my closest Manchester Grammar School friend Tommy Wagner (who had been killed flying a Fleet Air Arm Skua at Lee-on-Solent in January 1940) and R.T. Moore, who, as a Classics Master at MGS, had taught me to love Horace, Virgil and Cicero. A train came in and they were suddenly hidden from view.

It was the end of an era. In a few minutes we were on our way to Liverpool and Africa.

About the Author

Humphrey Wynn entered journalism under the Kemsley Graduate Training Plan. He served on newspapers in Manchester and London as a reporter/feature writer and in 1956 joined the aviation magazine *Flight*. In 1963 he went to the SBAC (Society of British Aerospace Companies) as Press and PR Officer, then in 1965 joined the Air League in a similar capacity. He returned to *Flight* in 1967 as Deputy Editor, then joined the Air Historical Branch of the Ministry of Defence in 1971 as a historian. While with the AHB he wrote *The Bomber Role, 1945-1970; The RAF Nuclear Deterrent Forces: their origins, roles and deployment 1946-1969 A Documentary History* (HMSO, 1994); and *Forged in War: A History of RAF Transport Command 1943-1967* (HMSO, 1996). He is also the author of other RAF titles like *Fighter Pilot: A Self-portrait by George Barclay* (William Kimber, 1976) and *Desert Eagles* (Airlife, 1993) and (with Susan Young) *Prelude to Overlord* (Airlife, 1983).

Acknowledgements

To all my wartime RAF contemporaries, whose friendships have lasted for a lifetime (No 2 Aircraft Delivery Unit held 50 successful reunions from 1947 to 1997); to Woodfield Publishing Ltd for their care, helpfulness and attention to detail; and to my dear amanuensis Kristina Sutton for retyping my original text so skilfully and preparing a disc.

H.W.

1.   To Africa

I shall never forget my first sight of Africa – thick green vegetation coming right down to the sea, or so it seemed from the rail of our troopship. Most of our group of 15 pilots had probably never been abroad before, or only on school trips. I had been to Paris and the Austrian Tyrol. Africa was something new, and we were about to disembark from the handsome SS *Duchess of Richmond*, in mid-October 1941, and sail along the West coast to Lagos in a much smaller vessel – the MV *Ulster Monarch*.

We had left Liverpool at the end of September, going far out into the Atlantic in a convoy guarded by the Royal Navy, whose brave and vigilant crews shepherded every RAF movement overseas during the war. We passed the days on those dark and angry waters playing housey-housey (as Bingo was then called), eating, smoking, sleeping – and chatting about what we were going to do when we got to wherever we were bound.

We knew vaguely that we were going to fly on the West African Reinforcement Route, from Takoradi to Cairo, and had been trained specially for that purpose. Instead of going to Operational Training Units on Blenheims or Wellingtons – as we all expected – some of us were posted to the Service Ferry Squadron at Kemble in Gloucestershire. There, much to our surprise, for we only had about 150 hours of flying experience altogether – on basic trainers like the Tiger

Moth or Magister or twin-engined ones like the Oxford or Anson, we got airborne in a variety of operational types like the Blenheim, Hurricane, Tomahawk and Maryland. As the Marylands had been destined for France, all their instrumentation was in French. However, we survived, possibly because ignorance was bliss, or maybe we had been well trained at our Elementary and Service Flying Training Schools.

Now here we were, nearly in sight of our destination – Takoradi – on what was then the Gold Coast (now Ghana). Nearly, but not quite: only a four-day haul in the *Ulster Monarch*, which plied before and after the war between Holyhead and Belfast. Now her destination was Lagos.

This voyage along the West African coast turned out to be a unique Odyssey, with only a very capable OC Troops preventing a mutiny; for MV *Ulster Monarch*, with about a thousand men on board, was not only unsuited for sailing in tropical waters but ran out of bread and meat and fresh water. The weather was hot and stormy and at night we slept up on the top deck – until we were caught and soaked in a tropical downpour.

Although we could see a protective corvette darting about and occasional depth charges going off, we didn't, at the time, realise the dangers faced by the Royal and Merchant Navies to get RAF personnel, aircraft and equipment to overseas theatres of war. At the time, after over three weeks at sea, we were only too glad to be setting foot on land again – a strange land, full of African faces and sounds.

Our group of pilots (and we had got to know each other pretty well by then) were lucky to be the first passengers to disembark, and we were taken to the Royal Hotel in Lagos – not as grand as it sounds, but my, white bread has never tasted so good! The lobby was a surge of native jabbering sounds and up on the roof garden there was jitterbugging to a gramophone. In the grounds there was a non-stop chirruping of crickets and, as night fell on our first day in Africa, we heard the croaking of bullfrogs all around the Apapa lagoon, under a velvety tropical darkness.

I wondered how long we would stay in Lagos, because I had a letter to deliver to my cousin Irene, who was working as a teacher at the CMS (Church Missionary Society) Girls' School there. As it happened, we had three days before a civil flight to Takoradi was available, so I took J D Taylor with me (we always knew him as "JD" and, like so many of my RAF pals, he was not to survive the war) and we received a very happy welcome from Irene – who'd sailed out earlier in 1941 – and her fellow teachers and pupils.

We flew from Lagos to Takoradi on 27 October by Lockheed Lodestar G-GBS of BOAC – a flight I chiefly remember because the passenger in front of me, who was wearing a Harris Tweed jacket, had a chameleon on his shoulder. This was the first time I had seen one of these small lizards at close quarters and I was fascinated by the creature's swivelling eyes, seemingly quite solid with a hole in the middle. I knew of its ability to change colour according to the local environment, but this one was hard put to imitate the green, brown and red flecks in its owner's jacket.

After an hour and forty-five minutes' flying, we landed at the whitewashed world of RAF Takoradi, on a black tarmac runway busy with Bristol Blenheims and Hawker Hurricanes being test-flown after being uncrated in the neighbouring docks and assembled by No 116 Maintenance Unit personnel. This was the "back door" for the aircraft reinforcements to the Middle East, based on pioneer flights by the RAF in the mid-1920s and 30s and a far-sighted decision in 1940 to create a string of staging-posts to Khartoum in the Anglo-Egyptian Sudan and thence to Cairo – a total distance of nearly 3,700 statute miles but free from enemy interference.

We soon found, however, that RAF Takoradi were not impressed by a group of young pilots who had only done 180-odd hours' flying. After three nights in the humid tropical Gold Coast climate – known by those posted there as "the white man's grave" – we were airborne again, once more as passengers, but this time going eastwards and northwards, to the desert sands of Egypt. This flight (or rather flights, for we changed aircraft at Khartoum) across Africa was one which I would not have missed for worlds – a real eye-opener for young men straight out from the confines of wartime Britain.

We were lucky in being flown up to Khartoum by Wing Commander W.E. Rankin, CO of No 117 Squadron which was based there – and with which I was to become much better acquainted later in its Western Desert days, in a

Douglas DC-2 – forerunner of the ubiquitous DC-3 Dakota which was to become so famous in Second World War years and for which I had great affection.

Seven years earlier, in the 1934 London-Melbourne air race for £15,000 in prize money put up by Sir Macpherson Robertson, a DC-2 flown by the Dutch pilots K.D. Parmentier and J.J. Moll had come second to the DH Comet *Grosvenor House,* piloted by C.W.A. Scott and T. Campbell Black. This was a notable achievement, because the DC-2 was a 20-seater commercial airliner, whereas the DH Comet – specially designed for the UK-Australia air race, had no commercial viability.

This Takoradi-Khartoum flight in DC-2 AX768 was the only experience I ever had of this type of aircraft, which served briefly in the Western Desert when No 117 Sqn were moved up there, before being replaced by the Lockheed Hudsons with which the squadron was re-equipped.

We first flew to Oshogbo (3hr 15min) in the south-west of Nigeria, north of Lagos, and I can still recall the majestic quiet of the tropical night there – a sort of peacefulness unknown in Europe. Then on the following day to Maiduguri in northern Nigeria (a 4hr flight), the thick vegetation of the south giving way to scrub and then the desert of mid-Africa.

Our third day's flying (5hr) took us into what was then the Anglo-Egyptian Sudan, to El Fasher; then on the fourth day we had a 3hr flight to our first destination – Khartoum. Approaching that city whose name is a legendary one in British Imperial history, I marvelled – as I was to do on many subsequent flights across Africa – at one of the great sights of the world, the confluence of the Blue and White Nile.

There was to be an even greater flying treat in store two days later (3 November), when we were passengers aboard the BOAC Short Empire flying-boat G-AFPZ *Clifton*, bound for Cairo via Wadi Haifa, for anyone who has not flown in this way has missed one of the most satisfying and comfortable forms of air travel.

First there was the experience of being ferried out across the Nile to get aboard. Then the running-up of each of the four Bristol Pegasus engines, the flying-boat swinging from side to side as power was applied. Then the take-off – the sensation first as of a speedboat, with spray lashing the windows as speed increased and the hull got "on the step" – then a sudden clearance from the water as *Clifton* got into her natural element and slowly climbed away, bound for Egypt's capital, with the Nile in view for most of the flight.

This is the way everyone should see Egypt for the first time, from the south, for that great river is her history and her geography.

In two "hops" – 3hrs to Wadi Haifa and 4hrs 15mins to Cairo – we cruised steadily at about 3,000 feet, and in the flying-boat's deep hull there was plenty of space to walk around and look through the windows at the Nile's winding course, the vegetation clinging to its banks and the endless desert on either side.

Egypt grows out of the Nile. The green cultivated area gradually increases on either side of the river; then the great sprawling modern capital – modern by comparison with the ancient cities like Thebes – gradually materialises, and beyond it the lush Delta area, broadening out towards Alexandria and the Mediterranean.

We landed smoothly on the Nile in the centre of Cairo, rocking gently to a noiseless rest, with white-sailed dhows and palm trees reminding us where we were as the BOAC launch came out to take *Clifton*'s passengers ashore. As RAF personnel of an undistinguished vintage, we were hurried off to transit accommodation. At least somebody in the Middle East Air Force knew we were coming. Or did they? Perhaps the signal from Takoradi had not yet arrived. Only the morning would tell us where we were going and what we were going to do – presumably get in some flying practice and increase our "hours" before doing our first trip up the 'Takoradi Route'.

It was 3rd November 1941 and we were about to be taken on the strength of MEAF – a vast Command stretching from West to North Africa and eastwards through Palestine and across the barren landscape of Iraq ~ territory with which we were to become familiar over the next three years.

2. A Taste of the Desert

We could not have had a better introduction to that Command when, the following morning, we met its Air Officer Commanding-in-Chief, Air Marshal Sir Arthur Tedder. Not by appointment, of course, but by fortuitous coincidence. We had gone to "book in" at Air Headquarters in Cairo and were waiting outside for one of our chaps to emerge. A staff car was parked by the pavement and Tedder came out. With commendable quickness born of recent drill and discipline training, Alfie Richbell yelled out: "Party, atten-shun!" and saluted.

Tedder, with that genius for informality which made him one of the Second World War's outstanding commanders, didn't rush past this undistinguished group of new arrivals but stopped to ask us where we had come from and when, and what we were going to do. When we said we were going to fly on the West African Reinforcement Route, he commented: "You are our lifeline" – words which summed-up the critical situation in the following year, when supplies of fighters and medium bombers via Takoradi and Accra were crucial to the Western Desert/Mediterranean air campaigns for which Tedder had ultimate responsibility.

For ourselves, getting experience of desert flying was the next step, and we were posted to No 1 Delivery Unit, which was based on LG 100 (all landing grounds in the Middle East theatre were numbered) at Wadi Natrun, midway between Cairo and Alexandria, a mile off the tarmac road which ran like a black thread through the desert to the west of the Nile delta area.

This was our first experience of several aspects of Middle East military life – transport by 30cwt desert-camouflaged "gharry" (as they were familiarly known), which had no discernable springing, hard bench seats along either side at the back and an awning which flapped at speed or in the wind; sandstorms, which blotted out everything and got into everything; "char" (tea), drunk from the broken-off lower half of brown Stella beer bottles at the Half Way House NAAFI (or whatever its proprietorship was) at Wadi Natrun; and sleeping in tents on the hard, stony sand.

But we were young, we were healthy; the climate was dry and invigorating: these strange new things were all now part of our way of life, and would be for the next three years.

What I did notice, and shall never forget, when darkness fell on that first night at Wadi Natrun, was the huge panoply of stars – right down to the horizon on every side. I couldn't help recalling Edward Fitzgerald's line in his marvellous translation of Omar Khayyam – *And that inverted Bowl they call the Sky* – an exact description of what we could see. No wonder the science of astronomy began in the Middle East.

Next morning we had our first full-focus view of LG100, which was, like all landing grounds in the Western Desert, a large, flat area of sand, its boundaries marked by empty oil drums; aircraft dotted about in a heat haze that would get hotter; the "desert lily" urinals made out of petrol cans; and Jill, an Alsatian who had the time of her life there.

I remember our first briefing by the Commanding Officer of No 1 Delivery Unit, Squadron Leader E M (Michael) Morris, a tall man of great charm, with a deeply lined face, sitting on the edge of a trestle table on which there was a field telephone – the sort you had to wind up. The role of No 1 DU was to get aircraft to the squadrons in the desert – wherever they might be – from the Maintenance Units in the Delta area. How they got there was up to the pilots, who then had to get themselves back to Wadi Natrun. This was a type of flying unique to the Western Desert, and depended greatly on individual skill and initiative.

Our "mentors" were a group of pilots who had been in the pre-war RAFVR and whom we therefore looked up to with great respect. They had mainly been on Bristol Blenheim squadrons in 1940-41. Tom Middleton, George McCarthy, Sam Fletcher and BE ("Tom") Brown were our respected heroes. All except Tom Middleton, who was killed on a Lancaster operation after he was posted back to the UK, survived the war and became lifelong friends (as did Michael Morris).

Surprisingly, in view of our recent emergence from wartime UK with its dark and Spartan existence, we adapted quickly to our new way of life. There was a healthy simplicity and informality about the Western Desert – although the major cities, Cairo and Alexandria, were within an hour's drive – which made it quite different from the formalised RAF life we had hitherto known. As we were to find during the next three years, the environment – and the personal initiative we could display in desert flying – conditioned our lives. But these were early days; we had yet to have many months' slogging up and down the West African Reinforcement route in disciplined convoys.

I had my first flight at Wadi Natrun with George McCarthy, a one-hour getting-to-know-the-area sortie in a Blenheim IV, the light bomber which suffered such terrible losses in France in 1940 and then on sorties across the North Sea. It became clear that with such simple geography and virtually cloudless skies there was little chance of getting lost. To the west was the road by which we had come from Cairo and the salt-producing lake, with its white shores and a factory chimney that was a useful indication of wind direction; to the east the dark green of the fertile Delta area; and to the north the Mediterranean coastline and Alexandria, with El Alamein still a little-known railway station and the ancient seaside resort of Mersa Matruh, beloved of Cleopatra, beyond it.

The following day – 15th November – I was airborne myself, for the first time since coming to Africa, in a Hurricane I – then the frontline fighter of the Middle East squadrons. I quickly learned the difference between flying in desert conditions and those of the UK, where there are plentiful landmarks for judging height; here the lack of them, plus the shimmering heat, produced some problems and caused some accidents – chaps "rounding out" too high on landing and stalling the aircraft. But we got used to this new environment; that's why we'd been sent to Wadi Natrun – to get acclimatised. I even did my first delivery trip (on the 23rd), flying a Hurricane I from No 108 Maintenance Unit south of Cairo – where I had been taken by Sergeant Taylor in a Blenheim IV – back to No 1 DU.

These MUs in the Delta area were keys to the supply of aircraft to the Desert Air Force, in the great reinforcement and rescue operation set up by Air Vice-Marshal Graham Dawson at Tedder's instigation. They not only received new aircraft ferried through the West African Reinforcement Route from Takoradi and Accra; they also rebuilt crashed machines retrieved from the Western Desert by the Repair and Salvage Units. The job of getting fighters and bombers from the MUs to the squadrons – now facing the Regia Aeronautica but soon to have much stiffer opposition from the Luftwaffe – was that of the ferry pilots, among whom my newly-arrived colleagues and I were the rawest of raw recruits, learning the trade from desert veterans (even if, in fact, they had only been at it for a few months; much depended on personal initiative in what was a freelance form of flying).

We were only to have two weeks at Wadi Natrun, because our job was to get back to Takoradi and fly aircraft up the West African Reinforcement Route, but in that time we got a taste of the Western Desert and also formed firm friendships.

I had a complicated first delivery flight "up the desert" in a Hurricane II, to LG103, then from there to Fuka, Gerawla and Sidi Heneish – I can't think why, but the experience must have given me some feel for that trackless desert terrain where so many battles were to be fought, and also in the art of getting a lift back to base, by whatever form of transport was available. I also took a Hurricane I to No 53 RSU (Repair and Salvage Unit) from No 103 MU at Aboukir, which was to become famous for adapting Spitfires to fly higher than they had ever flown before, in order to catch the Luftwaffe's high-flying Ju 86Ks on their daily reconnaissance sorties over Egypt from Crete. Before we left Wadi Natrun at the end of November I resumed acquaintance with the Curtiss Tomahawk, which I had flown on our conversion course at Kemble.

My special friendships were with J D Taylor (whom I've already mentioned), Geoff Mewies (who came from Holmfirth, the Yorkshire town near Huddersfield where his family had a laundry business and which was later to become famous as the setting for the TV series *Last of the Summer Wine*), Bob Smart (who had become engaged to "Midge" Hichisson, one of the girls whom we met at the dances we used to go to in the Corn Exchange at Chippenham when we were at Kemble) and Ken Prater (who in his pre-RAF days worked for the Michelin Tyre Company). Only Geoff and I survived to attend post-war reunions. "JD" was killed when instructing on Dakotas at Crosby-on-Eden; Bob came down, with several aircraft of the convoy he was leading, in swampland between Juba and Malakal in 1944; and Ken, who had become engaged to a South African girl in Cairo, crashed on take-off at Portreath in Cornwall, en route for Gibraltar, only a few days before VE Day in 1945.

When not flying we used to play bridge and I remember one afternoon when we were overwhelmed by a sandstorm that crept from the north, down the military road, blotting out everything in its path and filling the air inside the tent with tiny particles of dust.

But we were soon to leave the desert, with its normally clean, warm, dry, invigorating atmosphere. By the beginning of December 1941 we were on the way to West Africa to fulfil our designated role.

3.   Up (and Down) the Route

By now the West African Reinforcement Route was in full flow, with convoys of eight fighters (mainly Hurricanes at that time) led by a medium bomber (initially Blenheims) leaving Takoradi as soon as the aircraft had been assembled and test flown.

A policy decision had been taken to base the aircrew who were to do the flying not at Takoradi but in Cairo, where there were better recreational facilities between trips and where three Thomas Cook houseboats, used in balmier days for holiday trips up the Nile but laid up by Gezira Island for the duration of hostilities, were requisitioned as HQ and accommodation for the Aircraft Delivery Unit (Middle East) which was formed on 15 December 1941. Its offices were aboard *Medina* and the other houseboats used were *Egypt* and *Delta*. J D Taylor, Bob Smart and I made our way there from Wadi Natrun at the end of November, having done our short stint of desert flying at the Wadi Natrun Training Flight. We were to have a weekend in Cairo before leaving for Takoradi – initially by flying-boat – on 2nd December, the beginning of our "down and up" routine for the next 18 months.

Cairo, bursting with Service personnel of all nationalities – Australian, British, Canadian, Greeks, Palestinians, Rhodesians, South Africans and Yugoslavs – was all things to all men, a cosmopolitan city with a balmy climate, hot days and warm, star-studded nights, which catered for every human need – from gastronomic and physical to the basically sexual. Those who were stationed there, on the Headquarters staffs, managed to get themselves well organised according to their particular desires and habits. Young women in the ATS or WAAF had the time of their lives, with the male/female ratio steeply in their favour, and officers of Wing Commander/Lieutenant-Colonel rank or above could pick and choose when it came to women friends. Itinerant Sergeant Pilots like ourselves (although three of our course at Kemble had been commissioned – 'Maggie' Carter, 'Cabby' and Ron Barnard) were the lowest of the low in the aircrew pecking order but managed to find some modest pleasures, like swimming or tennis at the Gezira Club, the cinema and, of course, eating and drinking.

From the houseboat we could walk into the centre of Cairo, to its main streets like Suleiman Pasha, Sharia Emad el Din and Kasr el Nil. The warm climate meant that clothing was uncomplicated – shirts (or, better still, bush jackets) and shorts were the order of the day.

So was noise – car horns and Arabic curses, colour and variety, overloaded donkeys mixing with taxis in streets which flowed with constant movement.

On the Sunday evening (the last day of November 1941) Bob, Maggie and I went to Evensong in All Saints Cathedral – which had a full complement of Service personnel – and the next morning, laying up for myself treasure upon earth, I opened an account at Barclays Bank with £8. Then we rounded-off our first stay in the fleshpots (Alexandria was the other one, especially for Naval personnel) with two typical Cairo pastimes – the open-air cinema, where we saw Orson Welles in his classic *Citizen Kane* – and Groppi's, the restaurant which became synonymous with eating, drinking and meeting for wartime Allied military personnel of all ranks and a rendezvous for those who were about to return to the Western Desert or, in our case, to West Africa.

At seven o'clock the next morning, the BOAC Empire flying-boat *Cassiopaea* lifted off from the murky waters of the Nile in the middle of Cairo and, for the next six and three-quarter hours, we droned comfortably over the sites of Egypt's ancient history – the Pyramids of Gizeh, the Valley of the Kings, Karnak, Thebes and Luxor – and across the endless deserts of the Anglo-Egyptian Sudan, until we settled on the waters of the Nile again at Khartoum. There, we were taken to Wadi Seidna, an airfield some miles outside the city, which we were to see many more times over the next 18 months.

The RAF had had a station at Khartoum since the Imperial days of the 1920s. Wadi Seidna, on the other (Western) side of the Nile, was a red shale landing-ground developed to handle the ever-increasing flow of aircraft from West Africa, one of 163 staging posts around the world eventually created during the war to look after transit flights.

We came to know well those on the West African Reinforcement Route, and the service they provided always amazed me. For the ground crew it was a case of "they also serve who only stand and wait". At one moment there was silence, such as only Africa can provide, in the next the combined roar of a bomber and eight fighters, all of which had to be marshalled, serviced and refuelled and their crews given a meal or night-stop accommodation. Then they were off again, northwards to Egypt, and silence descended until the next convoy roared in out of the blue, breaking formation into an echelon starboard for landing.

We were to see the route in reverse for the first time that December morning – crossing southern Sudan, then the whole of Nigeria and along the West African coast from Lagos via Accra to Takoradi. The names of the landing-grounds became all too familiar – El Fasher, El Geneina, Maiduguri and Kano, almost the whole of the nearly 3,700-mile route being over British-controlled territory – though on occasions (yet to come) we landed at Fort Lamy in French Equatorial Africa.

On that morning of a six-fifteen departure from Wadi Seidna, another new experience awaited us – a flight by Pan American Airways, one of whose DC-3s was to take us to Takoradi. PanAm had been involved in the West African Reinforcement Route under a UK-US agreement signed in August 1941, to help cope with an increasing flow of American aircraft across the South Atlantic to Accra. Pan Am were thought in some quarters (notably by Air Marshal Tedder) to be Empire-building for post-war routes, though of course we knew nothing of such high matters at that time. We were brand-new ferry pilots, doomed for two days to fly as passengers.

There was plenty of time during the long flight (15 hours and five minutes, with a night stop at Kano) to study the terrain over which we ourselves would shortly be flying in single-engined aircraft. It was inhospitable, to say the least, in the event of a forced landing. The Sudan offered little but desert and scrubland; Nigeria meant bush and forests, often covered in low cloud. But we would be under the leadership of an experienced Blenheim pilot and his crew; all we had to do was to keep station in our convoy. I was to develop the utmost admiration for the aircraft captains, with their navigators and wireless operators, who led us across Africa without failing; for aids were few, and between Lagos and the Sudan (before the Nile provided visual guidance) some of the airfields were undistinguishable from the surrounding dusty terrain.

I was very impressed with Kano, a walled city with 12 gates – though the "wall" was made up of continuous lines of houses, which did not, in fact, completely surround the city. Their distinguishing features were a reddish-brown colour and little pinnacles on the corners of their roofs – in fact drainpipes, jutting out horizontally. These houses had low doorways, which sheep seemed to use as freely as their human inhabitants. This was our third look at an African city, first seeing something of Lagos after landing there and then getting acquainted with the noisy diversions and amenities of Cairo.

Our PanAm DC-3 (18117, with Captain Allison in command) staged via Lagos and Accra, and we landed at Takoradi just after half-past one on the afternoon of 4th December 1941, and when we got to the Mess, you could buy a bunch of bananas for a penny and a pineapple for 2d. As fledgling pilots, our usefulness to the RAF after a year's ground and air training was about to be put to the test.

The Maintenance Unit there, whose personnel worked in the enervating heat of a tropical climate with high humidity, had three main tasks: to unload the packing-cases brought in to the harbour by convoyed merchant ships and which contained fuselages, propellers and engines; to assemble these components into flyable fighters and bombers; and to test-fly and dispatch these aircraft to the Middle East for the Mediterranean campaigns.

We were attached to the Servicing Flight and no time was lost getting us into the air and off to Cairo. After a day on the ground (5th December, when pilots who had been on the third course at Kemble arrived by air from Freetown) I did an air test and an hour's practice flying on my "mount" (a Hurricane II with two 40-gallon overload tanks under its wings) and on the 7th Cabby, Maggie Carter and I left in No 281 Convoy. Our test flying had been done in the local area and, as usual, included a "beat-up" of the neighbouring village, Sekondi, and its palm-fringed beaches.

We would be relying on the well-proved Rolls-Royce Merlin engines to keep us airborne over thousands of miles during the next four/five days.

I remember thinking, as we flew eastwards towards Lagos, following the convoy leader in his Blenheim and with the West African coastline on our port side, 'Well, this is it; this is what we've been trained for.' What was then the Gold Coast and its main city, Accra, slid away, then there was a stretch of French West Africa and traces of earlier Portuguese settlements – white forts dotted along the shore, then, after two hours and 20 minutes' flying, we reached Lagos and landed at Apapa – a grass airfield about 1,000 yards long (or short, for inexperienced pilots such as we were), on the edge of the lagoon. Its limited length became more apparent the following morning when we took off with a full load of fuel (internal and external tanks) for the 3hr 10min flight to Kano, where, that afternoon, I enjoyed the gentle local recreation of some horse-riding.

In this two-day stretch to the middle of Nigeria we had covered 903 statute miles and I much admired the navigational skill of the crew in the Blenheim which led us. There was no problem about the first (Takoradi to Lagos) stage, but the second was a different matter. There was no question of map-reading over that vast terrain, the forested area thinning out into a trackless scrubland; everything depended on the navigator keeping a careful plot, aided by D/F (direction-finding) loop bearings obtained by the wireless operator and accurate course-keeping by the pilot. There were no automatic navigational aids and if the Blenheim (or whatever the lead aircraft was) strayed, a whole convoy could be lost. It is a tribute to these crews that this never seemed to happen. After hours of flying, with the steady African sun beating down on the white-painted Perspex cockpit cover, we would always see our destination airfield hove into view.

The next day's (9 December) progress eastwards was a much harder slog – six hours ten minutes all told – from Kano to Maiduguri, to El Geneina and thence to El Fasher, in what was then the Anglo-Egyptian Sudan. On that first occasion, Maiduguri and El Geneina were refuelling stops; but the contrast in accommodation between them and El Fasher, where we night-stopped, was extreme – between round mud huts with thatched roofs and pre-war Imperial Airways guest houses with wide, cool corridors enclosed by wire-mesh panels to provide fly-free ventilation, though not lion-free, for the groundcrew at El Fasher had adopted a lion cub which (not surprisingly, named Leo) who used to lie under the wings of convoy aircraft when they were lined up for refuelling. On one later occasion, rounding a corner in one of the wire-mesh corridors, I encountered Leo coming in the opposite direction and he rose on his hind legs and put his paws round my neck in friendly fashion – fortunately only a brief embrace. When he really got too big, Leo was transported to Khartoum Zoo. I hope he had a comfortable and trouble-free flight and that he lived on to a fine and much-respected old age.

The terrain between El Fasher and Wadi Seidna (Khartoum) was brown, barren and featureless, with a turning-point at El Obeid (where there was an emergency landing-ground) and thence north-eastwards to the great confluence of the White and Blue Nile rivers, an awe-inspiring landmark which moved me greatly when flying towards it for the first time – and on every subsequent occasion. Although in the Anglo-Egyptian Sudan, it seemed to be the historic gateway to the ancient land of Egypt, despite Cairo being another 1,000 miles to the north.

We had taken three hours to reach Wadi Seidna; from there to Wadi Haifa (one of the hottest places on earth – it was impossible to touch any metal parts of the aircraft when they had been standing out in the sun for refuelling, and cylinder head temperatures rocketed after take-off) was another two hours, 45 minutes' flying and after this fourth day there was another night-stop – so on that first occasion we had the advantage of taking-off in the cool of the morning.

On 11 December 1941, therefore, I completed my first delivery flight on the West African Reinforcement Route – two hours and five minutes to reach Luxor, that magnetic haunt of tourists in peacetime with its nearby Valley of the Kings and Thebes, and thence two hours 20 minutes to our destination – Kilo 8, a landing-ground eight kilometres north-east of Cairo, on the road to Suez.

Getting back to the house-boat by Gezira Island after five days' intensive flying and entirely new experiences was a relief, but we were not to relax for long. On the Saturday (13th) I sent off a Christmas greetings cable home and wrote my 14th letter to Father (all our correspondence was numbered, so we'd know if one letter failed to arrive) and the next day we were off again to Takoradi. This time our Short Empire flying-boat was VH-ABF *Cooee*, commanded by Captain Garner, in which we rumbled gently southwards for six and a half hours to Khartoum and from there again by Pan American DC-3 to Takoradi for a second convoy run.

We arrived there on 17th December for what was to be a West African Christmas, as we didn't leave on our second run until 7th January 1942, and I'll never forget the sound of the "boys" in the cookhouse of the Mess singing familiar carols as they worked – with that wonderfully natural sound and rhythm that Africans possess. I must confess that the music and words of "While shepherds watched", etc, in tropical surroundings, gave me a pang of homesickness.

1942 was to be a traumatic year for me – the last three trips in the genteel comfort of Empire flying-boats from Cairo to Khartoum (replaced by all-the-way-to-Takoradi PanAm DC-3s), four "prangs," conversion to a new type, malaria and sick leave – and a return to the Western Desert.

The "C" class flying-boats all had classical names – *Canopus* and *Camilla* were my last experiences of stately airborne progress from the Nile at Cairo to the Nile at Khartoum and as passengers aboard them and the PanAm DC-3s we could afford to take things easily for a few hours; it didn't much matter what had happened the night before, one could always "sleep it off on the plane" and besides, in one's 20s one seems to have astonishing powers of recovery.

On one return trip, with the usual stopover at Wadi Seidna, we went to a nightclub in Khartoum, a unique one because it was a rooftop establishment. What with the agreeable ambience – pretty girls of varied Middle East nationalities, plentiful liquid refreshment and subdued lighting under a star-spangled bowl of sky – I got very drunk in an enjoyable way. I remember climbing over from the back to the front seat of the taxi as we drove back to the Mess at an early hour and somebody must have helped to pour me into bed ... but we were up in time for take-off the following morning.

It was not, I think, on that flight but perhaps a later one that the captain of our PanAm DC-3 took it into his head to give us a spot of low flying after take-off from Fort Lamy, near Lake Chad in French Equatorial Africa (the only non-British-administered sector on the Takoradi route, with an airport runway made of red bricks). After getting airborne he climbed to only about 200 feet and followed the winding course of the River Sharia, whose muddy banks were festooned with hundreds of crocodiles, which slid into the dark water at the sound of the aircraft and as its shadow passed over them – a sight for tourists, perhaps, but a sick-making experience for its hapless passengers. However, we survived – back to Takoradi with its humid tropical air, so thick that I once watched a Bristol Beaufighter take off with its propeller tips cleaving through the atmosphere, sending back a cylindrical-shaped wash of vapour trails.

Two of my four "prangs" in 1942 were accidents for which I was responsible and rightly attributable to "pilot error"; the other two were the results of mechanical failure.

On 21st February, just two days after completing a Hurricane trip from Takoradi, I was sent off in a bright yellow North American Harvard, a two-seater trainer used by both the RAF and USAAF, one of a small convoy bound for Rhodesia. Unfortunately, I didn't get further than Luxor (a two-hour and 45 minute flight) because I ground-looped the aircraft on landing there, through over-correcting with the rudder.

American types had toe-actuated brakes on the rudder pedals and if these were actuated gently on the landing run, all was well. If one avoided using the brakes and attempted to steer the aircraft by the rudder pedals and it started to swing, over-correction would unlock the steerable tail-wheel (another feature of US types) and the aircraft would go into a swing; as this intensified, the undercarriage would collapse, and this is what happened to me at Luxor – to my great regret. My Flying Log Book was subsequently endorsed by the CO of the Aircraft Delivery Unit, Wing Commander Brian McGinn (who became a lifelong friend), but within three days I was back on the Takoradi route, leaving Heliopolis, that famous old airfield in the middle of Cairo, by PanAm DC-3 on the 24th.

This was for another Hurricane delivery trip, but after it there was to be a change of scene and of aircraft, the promise of new adventures and then a near-disaster, which, with its aftermath, put me off flying for seven weeks.

When I got back to Cairo on 21st March I was sent to the C and R (Conversion and Refresher) School at El Ballah, a landing-ground between the Sweet Water and Suez Canals, north of Ismailia and notable for its vast, white, salt-caked area, as smooth as the proverbial billiard table. Here I was to practice wheel landings – keeping the tail wheel off the ground for as long as possible until the speed decayed – in my old friend, the Harvard trainer and in a new type, the Curtiss P-40 Kittyhawk, an American fighter which would be used extensively in the Desert Air Force. But the destination of the first one I was to fly up the Takoradi route, a P-40E with USAAF markings, was quite different – the Flying Tigers of Major-General Clare Chennault in the China of Generalissimo Chiang Kai-shek.

But sometimes the great experiences of life elude us – by chance accident or some unlooked-for physical mishap – which is what happened to me. Going to China was one of those opportunities only wartime could offer; in the event, however, it was not an opportunity I was going to have … as will be told.

4. China-Bound – but Full-Stop Sharjah

We did our usual return trip to Takoradi by PanAm DC-3 at the end of March, then I was attached for a few days to the Test Flight, flying newly-erected Hurricanes and also getting rides in Blenheims with Warrant Officer Hallifax (who had a magnificent RAF handlebar moustache that he almost needed to retract before closing the cockpit hood in a single-seat aircraft) and Flying Officer Steele.

I flew a Hurricane II on 2nd April and the same day was sent by PanAm DC-3, with my convoy colleagues, to pick up USAAF P-40Es at Accra, which was the entry point for American aircraft to the West African Reinforcement Route. Our big adventure was about to begin, and when we left Accra on the 4th there was something new in store – the original Lagos landing-ground at Apapa, limited in area by its location on the edge of the lagoon, had been replaced by a new runway hacked out of the jungle some miles to the north, called Ikeja. This gave an appreciably longer landing and take-off run and our P-40Es, with their white star USAAF markings, roared off from there on 8th April in a convoy bound for China, initially led by Flying Officer Paynter.

We had a night stop at Maiduguri in northern Nigeria and another at Fort Lamy in French Equatorial Africa, two highly contrasting locations. Transit accommodation at the former was of the most primitive kind – thatch-roofed mud huts. When the Americans came to use the West African Reinforcement Route in 1942, they flew in and erected prefabricated metal buildings and their amenities included a PX (public exchange), that all-purpose type of store (groceries, sweetshop and chemist) which existed on USAAF bases and which, at Maiduguri, was much patronised by the RAF.

Fort Lamy, the only landing-ground on the route which was not on British-administered territory, offered a passing insight into the French colonial system, which tolerated much closer and more intimate relations with the native inhabitants – and any transit RAF aircrew delayed there for more than one night for bad weather or unserviceability reasons had to beware that bar stocks were more characterised by liqueurs like Creme de Menthe, Benedictine or Grand Marnier than by good old English beer.

Although our flight from Maiduguri took only 55 minutes, we night-stopped at Fort Lamy. While I didn't realise it at the time, this would have been an "operational delay" imposed by the controlling authorities – No 203 Group at Khartoum and No 202 Group at Heliopolis, Cairo – to avoid convoys "bunching up" and overcrowding the servicing and catering/accommodation facilities at individual Staging Posts.

From Fort Lamy, eastwards and northwards, our route was the traditional one – El Geneina, El Fasher, Wadi Seidna, Wadi Halfa and Luxor – but then, instead of the fighters parting company with their leader and heading for

Maintenance Units, the entire convoy landed at Ismailia for a transit stop. This airfield, by Lake Timsah, was distinguished by its exceptionally wide, black tarmac runways – an historic visual reminder of those days in 1937 when two Vickers Wellesleys (single-engined monoplanes with a 74ft 7in wingspan) of the RAF Long Distance Flight took off from there to fly non-stop to Australia, more than 6,000 miles away, a feat they just achieved before their fuel tanks ran dry.

We had a five-day break and took off again on 17th April with a new convoy leader, Warrant Officer Noble. We were now to cross territory I had never seen before – Palestine, Iraq (which used to be called Mesopotamia) and the Persian Gulf, most of it barren and featureless desert lands, but well known to the British Army and the RAF.

It took an hour to reach Aqir and I felt a strange sensation at setting foot on what we used to call, in childhood Sunday School days, 'The Holy Land' – which I was to see again, sooner than I thought and in much more detail. From there, a 2hr 30min leg to Habbaniyah, the great RAF base in mid-Iraq, a key staging-post on the Imperial route from Egypt to India since the 1920s.

We arrived over the airfield in style, roaring across it in close formation, then breaking off for a stream landing. Our overnight accommodation was not so stylish; we had to sleep, not very comfortably, in a gymnasium Next morning we were off again – to Shaibah, the RAF base at the head of the Persian Gulf, which in the 1920s, '30s and '40s was the inspiration for so many ribald songs and sayings and the origin of the *Shaibah Blues*[1] – but we were not to reach there on our first go – the convoy had to return to Habbaniya after 35 minutes' flying because the Blenheim's wireless was unserviceable. Our second, successful, attempt took an hour and a half and we night-stopped at this famous (or infamous) RAF station.

The next day (20 April) was Doomsday for me. There was no problem about the half-hour flight to Kuwait's dusty airfield, but my landing at Bahrain nearly spelt the end of my RAF service – and of me.

I came in to land much too fast, and had it not been that there was endless room – no runway, but acres of flat, hard salt-caked surface – I would have come to grief, probably finishing-up upside-down. As it was, I managed to corkscrew my way through a scrubby landscape as my speed diminished, then taxied back to where the other aircraft in the convoy were lined up for refuelling.

No-one seemed to regard the incident as anything other than an error of judgement, and after the usual transit stop we took off again for the two hour and five minutes flight down the Gulf to Sharjah – which, unlike the large, flat island of Bahrain was a concentrated area of a soft gravel airfield hard by a picturesque fort. Clearly, at some time in the 1920s and '30s, the natives had been less than friendly.

Fortunately, I landed my P-40E (5702) quite normally, but that day, 20th April, saw the end for me of the

---

[1] This song, plus many other favourites enthusiastically performed by RAF personnel all over the world, is to be found in *Bawdy Ballads & Dirty Ditties of the Wartime RAF*, published by Woodfield Publishing Ltd.

adventure of flying from Africa to China. I was taken off the convoy and sent to the Station Sick Quarters, where the Medical Officer's diagnosis was that I had sand-fly fever.

There were only two of us in the ward where I was put to bed, and my neighbouring bedfellow looked so dreadful I could hardly tell whether he was alive or dead. Not that I fared much better, for two days later the MO concluded that I had had heatstroke. Then the final blow fell; the poor fellow in the next bed had the screens put up around him, then disappeared (whether for better or worse I never knew) and on the 25th I was diagnosed as having malaria – which meant lots of quinine.

It meant, also, a move to a proper RAF hospital – so on the 25th I was taken to Abu Dhabi – an island off the coast south-west of Sharjah where there was a flying-boat base – and from there I was flown by one of BOAC's stately "C" class flying boats (this time *Canopus*) back up to Bahrain, which took two and a half hours, then a further 2½ hours up the Gulf to Margil, near Shaibah, where I was put into hospital – a stay which lasted for just over three weeks before I was adjudged fit enough to return to Cairo and (after sick leave) resume flying duties.

While I have no "recollection of things past" about those weeks in hospital, I'm grateful to the doctors and nurses who treated me and got me over malaria (an affliction which used to cause consternation when I became a blood donor in post-war years, because "malaria" was stamped on my card, though I never had a recurrence), but I do recollect with clarity my journey back from Basrah to Cairo on 18th May 1943, because it was again made by stately flying-boat, and my subsequent sick leave in Palestine.

What distinguished the flight in BOAC Empire flying-boat *Castor,* made in three stages, was that it included a landing on the Dead Sea, 1,300ft below sea level and extending north and south, which, with tawny mountains to the east, meant a long, straight descent and subsequent toiling climb-out in the hot air.

We had originally taken off from the river at Margil, the Shatt-el-Arab, and flown across the desert to Habbaniyah, where we landed on the lake, one of the remarkable and valuable attributes of that great base, which, in addition to its landing and maintenance facilities, had the amenities and accommodation of a city. From there to Kallia on the Dead Sea – a long toil that took three hours and 40 minutes – then we had a further two hours' flying before touching down on the Nile – by now a familiar destination.

My flying for May – only eight hours as a passenger – was signed for in my Log Book by Squadron Leader J.H. ("Red") Williams as Acting OC, Aircraft Delivery Unit, RAF Middle East, whom I then hardly knew personally – though he had an exuberant reputation – but who later became a lifelong friend. He had been in the theatre since before the war, had served on a Blenheim squadron (No 45) in the Western Desert and was later to command No 2 ADU, responsible for all aircraft deliveries in the Mediterranean area.

He signed my Log Book in his office aboard the houseboat *Medina,* one of the three ex Thomas Cook vessels (the others were *Egypt* and *Delta*) moored off Gezira Island, and sent me off on sick leave. Where was I to go? There was only one possible destination – Palestine. And how was I to get there? Only one way for a junior Sergeant Pilot – by train from Cairo to Tel Aviv. So another of life's adventures – an unlooked-for one – began for me when I set off, on 21st May, from Egypt to the Promised Land, following in Moses' footsteps, though he and the Israelites had had to walk all the way.

When you realise what it must have been like for those hundreds of dusty feet, you appreciate that one of man's greatest achievements was the invention of the wheel – and an even greater one, that of the aeroplane, which can skim over hundreds of miles of desert in a few hours. On that May afternoon, however, I was confined to a one-dimensional form of transport – the train – a confinement which lasted for nearly 17 hours, for we chuffed out of the noisy pandemonium of Cairo Station at ten to three in the afternoon and got to Tel Aviv at 7.42 the following morning – crossing the Suez Canal at El Kantara (which an aunt of mine, who'd been a nurse with Allenby's Army in the First World War, had often told me about) and chugging up the coast, with the blue Mediterranean on our left-hand side.

From the time I signed-in at Talbot House, a Toc-H hostel in Hayakon Street, a new world awaited me in the dry, clear air of this small country which has had such a monumental impact on human civilisation.

It was an ideal place in which to convalesce, not only because of the healthy climate but because there was so much to see, and within easy reach. I enjoyed the physical pleasures of Tel Aviv, its beach (in perpetual sunshine), its restaurants – especially an Austrian one where I was introduced to Wiener Schnitzel (and also to Vodka, through meeting a Polish officer) and the aesthetic pleasures of visiting places that Sunday School afternoons and lessons read in Church had made legendary – making far-off names and scenes from the Old and New Testaments come alive.

I saw the wells where Elijah was fed, saw where David killed Goliath, visited Bethlehem, went down to the Dead Sea again and in Jerusalem made my pilgrimage to those sites revered over many centuries – the Garden of Gethsemane, the Via Dolorosa and the Wailing Wall. I also went northwards, to Samaria, Mount Tabor, Nazareth, Tiberias, Mount Carmel and Haifa. After two weeks, with a mind full of wonderful and unforgettable sights and a body restored to health and vigour, I took the train from Tel Aviv for the long trundle back to Cairo – and a return to flying.

It was early June 1942 and this was to be a crucial year for the Allies in the Western Desert, with the Afrika Korps soon to begin its final offensive into Egypt, which would bring it to El Alamein to meet a concentration of 8th Army and Desert Air Force units behind that defensive line.

What the DAF needed was every aircraft it could get via the West African supply route and from another shipping terminal – Port Sudan on the Red Sea.

5. Return to the Route

I was instructed to join a convoy from there, to fly up some Curtiss Kittyhawks (P-40s), and on 7th June we left Cairo by road for Bilbeis, a big sandy airfield on the edge of the Delta area and just east of the Ismailia Canal. I came to know it well in a couple of years' time, when it was used for conversion training. We were due to fly down to Summit, the airfield for Port Sudan, by Lockheed Lodestar, but when we overshot, and in back-tracking saw the Lodestar take off, we thought that things had gone wrong and we'd missed our flight. However, it turned out that the pilot, Squadron Leader Taylor, was doing some "circuits and bumps" (take-off and landing practice), presumably for the benefit of his co-pilot, so we were able to leave in due course and, after four hours 40 minutes' flying, we landed at Summit.

I shall never forget my first sight of the blueness of the Red Sea, fringed by the Nubian Desert and tawny-arid mountains on its Western side – a dry, formidable area. We were supposed to leave on the following day, but the Martin Baltimore which was to lead us (flown by Squadron Leader Ruston) was unserviceable, and there was a dusty, harmattan-like wind, so a spelling and general knowledge "bee" was organised for the pilots, in which, I may say, the airmen beat the officers.

Take-off on the morning of 9th June was a strange sensation after being off flying for seven weeks, but nothing untoward occurred on the first leg (two hours over very inhospitable terrain) to Wadi Halfa, where, like a branch line, we joined the main Takoradi-to-Cairo reinforcement route. There was a railway from Port Sudan to Atbara on the Nile and, provided contact was maintained with it and the river, aircraft were comparatively safe in the event of a forced landing.

Only a month before, on 9th May, a Polish Air Force pilot (one of many who flew on the West African reinforcement route), Flight Sergeant Ignacy Mikolajczak, had had to force land his Kittyhawk after running out of fuel when he lost contact with three other Kittyhawks and became disorientated in a sandstorm. These three aircraft were successfully put down near Luxor and their pilots rescued, but Mikolajczak was a thousand miles south-south-east of Wadi Halfa when he forced-landed – without damaging his Kittyhawk – and died of thirst before he could be rescued, after keeping a diary of his last days.

Our flight from Wadi Halfa to Luxor (an hour and 20 minutes) and from there to No 107 Maintenance Unit at Kasfareet on the Bitter Lake (an hour and 40 minutes) was routine. We went back from there to Cairo by road.

During this year (1942) the West African Reinforcement Route reached its climacteric, reflecting the 8th Army's fighting retreat to El Alamein and the build-up of Desert Air Force and ground armament for the final offensive to drive the Afrika Korps back to Tripoli, on to Tunis and out of Africa.

I was to have two-and-a-half more months on the route before a change occurred at the beginning of September, and during that time I had three "mishaps", two of them mechanical and the other partly of my own making. Also, we were denied the luxury of a stately flying-boat ride from Cairo to Khartoum; on 11th June and on subsequent occasions it was a Pan American DC-3 which took us all the way from Almaza, the Cairo civil airport, to Takoradi.

The mechanical mishaps happened in July, oddly enough within six days of each other. On the 2nd, when landing a Kittyhawk at El Fasher, its port oleo leg collapsed, although my instrument panel indicated "three greens", meaning that the main and tail wheels were all locked down. Then, on the 8th, preparing to land a Hurricane at Kano, I found I couldn't lower the undercarriage. Perhaps if I'd had greater confidence I might have inverted the aircraft and tried the undercarriage lever while the weight was off the locks, but the Hurricane was burdened with two overload fuel tanks.

I flew around as long as possible to make sure that the fuel in them was exhausted, then landed on them – like a sort of dual skid – along the grassy side of Kano's red shale runway. There was no fire (though I hopped out pretty smartly) and little damage was done to the aircraft.

The third mishap occurred at Fort Lamy, on the day before my undercarriage collapse at El Fasher, when I was in the circuit before landing and wound back the cockpit hood – inside of which a sort of fluting in the metal fuselage provided a useful storage space, where I'd stowed a briefcase containing a camera, books and maps, all valuable possessions, which the slipstream whisked away. I tried unavailingly to find them on the ground after landing – they were probably located one day subsequently by an astonished, and perhaps delighted, Chad local inhabitant – or perhaps they remain undiscovered to this day.

Dropping out of a convoy through misadventures like an undercarriage failure usually meant back-tracking to Takoradi. After my Kittyhawk mishap at El Fasher I was sent back to Kano and stayed there for two weeks, air-testing two "repaired" Hurricanes and taking the second one on in a convoy to Cairo.

This was to be my very last trip up the Takoradi route, and it was coloured by an unexpected colonial interlude – a five-day stay at Fort Lamy – because a panel flew open on my Hurricane on take-off and I had to return, then wait for the next convoy coming through.

As I mentioned earlier, the French colonialists seemed to integrate themselves more closely with the native population than was the case with their British counterparts in Africa, at least, that's how it seemed to me. I've also mentioned the plentiful stocks of liqueurs in the Officers' Mess bar, and I recall in detail a typical menu at the Airport Hotel:

Fried Eggs; Jam; Bread;
Coffee
Salad Eggs; Fish;

Chicken, Beans, Peas;
Lettuce; Roll and Jam;
Coffee;

Soup; Watercress;
Toast and Kidney on "Sticks;"
Meat, slices of Toast and "Veg;"
Lettuce; Roll with Rum flavouring;
Coffee

Clearly there was ample time for me to copy those details down in my diary; there was nothing to do each hot day but wait for the word that a convoy was coming through. At last it came, and on 2nd August I was off – never to see Central or West Africa again.

But this last trip "up the route" was not without its special experience – a stay of 11 days at El Geneina on the Chad/Sudan border – for what reason I cannot recall, but probably an "operational" delay, perhaps ordered by Group Headquarters (No 203 Group at Khartoum) because of overcrowding of accommodation and pressure on facilities further up the route.

I remember that the airmen at El Geneina had a pet cheetah – quite delightful while it retained the dimensions and disposition of a domestic cat. I remember also wandering round the airfield perimeter (where an unfortunate Vickers Wellington in transit had overshot and ended up on its nose) and seeing a native shepherdess, naked to the waist, with her flock of goats with their tinkling bells. In her simplicity, in the great silence all around, she seemed to symbolize primitive Africa – a world now gone for ever.

As it happened, the Hurricane I was flying (a Mk II – BP443) had to be delivered to Gaza in Palestine, involving a refuelling stop at LG224 (Cairo West airfield, which I later came to know well) on the Cairo-Alexandria military road. I couldn't help recalling that line from John Milton's *Samson Agonistes,* which I'd read at school: '*Eyeless in Gaza at the mill with slaves'.* Gaza was then a quiet Arab town, long before it acquired its later notoriety.

How was I to get back to Egypt? Well, in a routine which was to become familiar, I delivered another Hurricane (in later days it could be any type of aircraft) to Wadi Natrun, with which I had become acquainted during the previous autumn, and in the interim I had been posted to another unit – No 1 Section, Aircraft Delivery Unit – which in July had moved to Abu Sueir, an historic RAF airfield about ten miles west of Ismailia, on the Ismailia Canal.

My apprenticeship days – flying in convoys up and down the West African Reinforcement Route – were over. I was about to be introduced to a very different kind of ferrying, up and down the Western Desert, in which personal initiative was paramount. None of the pilots knew from one day to the next what they would be flying, or where. These sorts of operations were peculiar to the Middle East Air Force and the Mediterranean area in particular; they had never occurred before in the RAF and would never occur again. Having done a routine apprenticeship, I was gradually to become a professional, through hard-won experience in 1942-43, as will be recounted.

6. Abu Sueir Interlude

In pre-war days, many fledgling RAF pilots had got their first taste of the air at No 4 Flying Training School at Abu Sueir, to which they were posted from the UK to make steady airborne progress in the unvarying Egyptian climate, far from the unstable vagaries of British weather. The station had brick-built accommodation and tarmac runways, and at that time in 1942 – when the whole of the Desert Air Force was concentrated in the Delta area, behind the El Alamein line – housed three squadrons in addition to ourselves: Nos 37 and 70 with Wellingtons, whose main task was to pound nightly the ports which supplied the Axis forces – Benghazi and Tripoli, and No 89 with night-fighter Beaufighters.

The "Wimpies" (as the Wellingtons were always known after the cartoon character Wellington J Wimpy) would pound along the runway, noses down and tails up as they struggled to gain flying speed; for these were ageing Mk 1s powered (or rather, underpowered) by Bristol Pegasus engines. The Beaufighters had a special fascination because the squadron was commanded by a legendary RAF character, Wing Commander G.H. (George) Stainforth, who in 1931 had set up a new world airspeed record of 407.5 mph in a Supermarine S.6B seaplane after the British team had won the Schneider Trophy outright.

Stainforth was an authoritarian CO, not universally liked by his crews, but he was a superb pilot – able to slow-roll a Beaufighter in the airfield circuit and keen to fly any new type of aircraft he could lay his hands on, including those held on temporary charge by No 1 Section, ADU, whose CO (Squadron Leader 'Red' Williams) became adept at finding unexpected causes of unserviceability – which rendered them unfit to fly – whenever Stainforth came snooping around on the lookout for something of interest.

It was after Flight Lieutenant John Boothman had captured the Schneider Trophy for Great Britain that the then Flight Lieutenant Stainforth had set up a new world airspeed record (407.5 mph – 655 kph) in the same Supermarine S.6B. Later in his career, in 1938 when he was OC the Handling Flight at the Central Flying School at RAF Upavon, he received the first Spitfire to be delivered to the RAF. It was flown in by test pilot Jeffrey Quill, who subsequently described this momentous event in his autobiography *A Test Pilot's Story*,[2] recalling that Stainforth – whose Flight had the responsibility of writing Pilot's Notes on new types for the squadrons – was "greatly intrigued" by the Spitfire.

At Abu Sueir, Stainforth was a distinguished Wing Commander who held the Air Force Cross for his pre-war flying achievements. He had formed No 89 Sqn in the UK and brought it out to the Middle East for night-fighter duties. Tragically, on the moonlit night of 27 September

---

2. Published by John Murray in 1983 and in paperback by Crécy Books, 1998.

1942 he and his navigator Pilot Officer Lawson were killed when they baled out, at too low an altitude for their parachutes to deploy fully. Their Beaufighter (X7700) came down one mile west of Gharib in the Delta area.

A friend of mine, Don Anderson, who had been on No 2 ADU but was temporarily downgraded for medical reasons, was then on the strength of a GCI (ground-controlled interception) unit known as an AMES (Air Ministry Experimental Station – a cover name) in the Fayoum area at that time. In post-war correspondence he told me: "We had a Lysander[3] which I recall flying over the area to find the crashed aeroplane. Through the grapevine it had been inferred that Stainforth had crashed in an unknown area, although from what I have learned since, this was incorrect. At the time, I recall that I thought that how could a pilot of such experience over so many years perish in so simple an accident. It was out of character."

He added that "the bodies were recovered and the crashed aircraft had not caught fire. It appears that no Court of Inquiry was held ... and nothing official has been properly determined [though] many suggestions have been made as to the cause [of the accident]."

Abu Sueir was my first experience of a fully organized RAF station, after the yo-yo existence of the Takoradi-Cairo reinforcement route, with its floating HQ on the Nile houseboats RS *Delta, Egypt* and *Arabia*, which were moved up river in July 1942.

---

3. Westland Lysander, a slow-flying, short take-off and landing high-wing monoplane.

We were there because this was a time of crisis in Egypt, with the Afrika Korps still advancing eastwards – to be held in the Battle of Alam Haifa at the end of August 1942 – and the Allied forces withdrawn into the Delta area, to be regrouped for the decisive Battle of El Alamein.

What those of us who were mere footsoldiers at that time – NCO pilots with only a few months' productive flying experience – did not realise was that we were part of a huge aircraft supply and reinforcement organisation, set up by the foresight, and under the aegis of, the AOC-in-C Air Marshal Tedder.

Not long after he had been posted to the Middle East in 1941 he had brought out from the UK, with that dour insistence of which he was capable, Air Vice-Marshal Graham Dawson as Chief Maintenance and Supply Officer – an entirely new appointment which ruffled a few Establishment feathers. A forceful character, both a pilot and an engineer, Dawson knew what he wanted and was not afraid to tread on a few corns to get it. Working through No 206 Group, which controlled all the Maintenance Units, he reorganised and revitalised the whole system of the supply of aircraft to the Desert Air Force. The MUs prepared new aircraft for operational service, and the RSUs (Repair and Salvage Units), which were mobile and backed-up the squadrons, ensured that the DAF was supplied – either with brand-new machines or ones which were sent back to the Delta area for refurbishing, having become operationally unserviceable ("clapped out" was the term) or having crashed and been picked up. We in No 2 ADU (Aircraft Delivery Unit), as our unit became from 3 December 1942, were part of this organisation, and operationally we were controlled by No 216 Group – the Ferry and Transport Group set up in May 1942, which had a charismatic AOC (Air Officer Commanding), Air Commodore Whitney Straight, who had had a heroic bout of operational experience before he took up his new appointment in September 1942 – to the chagrin of some well-established senior officers in Cairo; for the new AOC (who had "escaped and evaded" after being shot down over France in August 1941 and repatriated in August 1942) was still only a substantive Flight Lieutenant. But, like that of Graham Dawson, his appointment was a wise and imaginative one.

American born, Whitney Straight had made his mark before the war in motor racing and light aviation, as an aircraft designer and pilot; he served in the Auxiliary Air Force and by 1942 had twice been decorated – with the Military Cross as a liaison officer with the Army during the ill-fated Norwegian campaign of 1940, when he organised local labour to clear the frozen-lake airfield at Lesjeskog of snow so that the Gladiators of No 263 Sqn could land on it, and with the Distinguished Flying Cross for his command of a Spitfire squadron (No 242) in sweeps over France during 1941, when he was shot down but evaded capture and got back to the UK in August 1942 – being then precipitated to his new Command, which was responsible for a vast area and involved multiple activities.

In its transport operations No 216 Group was responsible to Headquarters, Middle East Air Force, and gave close support to the Desert Air Force squadrons. In its ferry operations the Group supported No 206 Group, which controlled the Maintenance Units (and BARU – the British Airways Repair Unit) in the Delta area, and the Repair and Salvage Units, which were mobile and had a dual function – to supply the DAF squadrons and to get time-expired or damaged aircraft back to the MUs for refurbishment. No 2 ADU provided the flying links in this reinforcement process – taking operationally-ready machines from the MUs to the RSUs and squadrons, wherever they might be in the Western Desert or beyond, and bringing back the battle casualties (those which were flyable). If 2 ADU pilots could not fly themselves back to base, they were picked-up by the unit's Hudson or Anson aircraft, which came to form what was in effect a small airline.

The Unit's aims were versatility and ubiquity: its pilots had to be able to fly any type of aircraft used in the Middle East/Mediterranean theatre (in fact it handled 49 different types) and deliver them wherever they were required. Its operational area stretched from Gibraltar in the west to India in the east; and in addition to No 1 ADU which flew the West African Reinforcement route, two more ADUs were formed in 1943 – No 3 at Fez, Morocco, to ferry aircraft from Casablanca to Cairo after the Axis forces had been driven out of Africa; and No 4 at Azizia, south of Tripoli, to reinforce the squadrons in Sicily and Italy.

7.   Up the Desert

The autumn/winter months of 1942-43 were historic ones for the 8th Army and the Desert Air Force, with the Battle of El Alamein and subsequent break-out and advance westwards. For support units like No 2 ADU, which until 3 December was still No 1 Section, ADU, there were corresponding changes.

On 26 November it had moved southwards from Abu Sueir, after four and a half months there, to LG209, a large area of sand on the north side of the Cairo-Suez road. Unlike Abu Sueir with its long-established accommodation, there was nothing there; tents were the order of the day.

I remember that when the first aircraft landed the *fellahin* (Egyptian peasants) were still smoothing out the runway with their brooms. They had no conception of how dangerous aircraft were.

It was amazing how, given the right domestic equipment, the RAF could get organised in that benign climate. In addition to No 1 Section, ADU, there was an ARP (Aircraft Reinforcement Park) and the flow of aircraft to the DAF squadrons was hardly interrupted by the move. Just before it, on the 24th, 24 Spitfires had been delivered to Gazala, and shortly after it, on the 29th, 16 Bostons were flown to Tmimi. These names of desert landing grounds were very familiar to us but have long been forgotten.

Changes of name and command also occurred at this time, No 2 ADU coming into being on 3rd December, directly under the control of No 216 Group. A couple of days later there was a big send-off party for Squadron Leader Michael Morris, who had opened-up LG 100 on the Cairo-Alexandria road at Wadi Natrun when the original Western Desert ferry unit, No 1 DU, had been formed. Combining authority with charm, he was going off to command the prestigious No 216 Squadron. His successor at No 2 ADU, who arrived to take over on the 7th, was Squadron Leader J H ("Red") Williams AFC.

"Red," who had acquired his nickname because of his auburn hair, was a very experienced Middle East pilot. He had flown Blenheims on No 45 Squadron in the Western Desert and had led convoys up the Takoradi route – his first in January 1941 and his last in January 1942, and on one occasion, when he had his neck in plaster as the result of a flying accident (described by Charles Graves in his book *The Avengers,*[4] where he wrote that, "every pilot in the Middle East had autographed the plaster ... and most of them had at some time or another poured a drink down the aperture.")

When "Red" took over command the variety and range of 2 ADU operations was steadily increasing. By the end of November its pilots had delivered 7,206 aircraft; it handled every type which came into the Middle East theatre (Flight Lieutenant Colin Glen evaluated each new one to provide

---

4. Published by Hutchinson & Co.

handling notes for the unit), and as the 8th Army and the Desert Air Force squadrons moved Westwards, the longer were the delivery flights and the time needed for pilots to get back to base.

I had one lucky break in December, which was to help me in what was to come. On the 17th I was sitting in the Mess, half-heartedly turning over the pages of a *Saturday Evening Post*, when suddenly old "Jumbo" Tanner came in and asked me if was keen to fly the Anson. A well-built, genial character who sadly later "bought it" in an accident, he'd recently been binding away pretty consistently for two things – to fly a Spitfire and "twins." He went on to explain that, finding himself at a loose end, he has asked Flight Lieutenant "Sticky" Glew (who was in charge of training and conversion) if he could go round in the Anson – "faithful Annie," the onetime frontline Coastal Command type which the unit used for transporting pilots to MUs in the Delta area and picking them up after delivery flights, when the number of passengers it carried would have astonished its designers.

"Sticky" Glew seemed to prefer to sit in a chair in the sunshine reading a book on this particular morning, rather than to be bothered with flying, but having been badgered sufficiently by Flight Sergeant Tanner, agreed to give him some dual – if he could find two or three more keen types. Well, I jumped at the opportunity, so we found another chap and renewed the offensive, whereupon "Sticky" Glew, still engrossed in his book but recognising that his conditions had been fulfilled, laid down another one – that if we could get the engines of AW854 (the ropeyest of the unit's Ansons) started, he would give us some dual.

We did, and though he still had to be prised out of the Mess, "Sticky" gave us an hour and 20 minutes' dual, during which we each did two "circuits and bumps." That was in the morning; in the afternoon we went up by ourselves, practising single-engined flying and doing more take-offs and landings. It was a pleasant change to fly a twin-engined machine again, and a month later I got another opportunity, flying a Bisley (Blenheim V) out of Heliopolis to Abu Sueir. The only Blenheim I had previously flown was a short-nosed Mark I at Kemble in September 1941.

This little interlude cast its shadows before; in a few weeks my flying experience was to change radically, when I became a multi-type pilot, but in the days after our "Sticky" Glew encounter I had two notable experiences: one probably the most interesting and the other certainly the most exciting of any that I'd had during the war.

On 18 December six of us were detailed to go up to Gazala, west of Tobruk, to help in moving No 53 RSU (Repair and Salvage Unit) there to a new site at Magrun, about 48 miles south of Benghazi on the main road. This meant ferrying the aircraft to their new base; we were due to make two trips each.

We took off in Hudson V9037, flown by Flight Lieutenant A B R Dow, and on the three-hour trip I passed the time studying a map of where we were to fly the Kittyhawks/Warhawks (the Packard Merlin powered version) and reading a copy of the *Saturday Evening Post* which I'd snaffled from the Mess.

I sat first in the wireless operator's seat, but it became pretty hot there, so later I retired to the back of the aircraft and lay down on a sleeping bag on top of a parachute. Soon, under the influence of the warm sunshine through the aircraft windows, I put down the magazine and dozed into semi-consciousness. Some time afterwards I sat up to see where we were; we were over Gazala III landing-ground; it was almost 10-45. When we landed we found that our "mounts" were ready to go. We signed the Form 700s (filled in by all the relevant trades – fitter, rigger, armament, instruments, etc – to certify that the aircraft was serviceable) and climbed aboard the gharry which would take us to the adjoining LG, Gazala II. I found that my aircraft was a Warhawk and was the second pilot to take off.

I followed the coastal road to Martuba and having circled Martuba West LG set a course of 270°. My altimeter was reading 2,500ft but I was flying less than 500ft above the tops of the hills; fortunately, visibility was excellent. The countryside in the Cyrenaican 'bulge' was green and undulating – a very pleasant change from the completely desert land extending eastwards up to the cultivated area of the Nile delta. The numerous small hills were covered with a sort of coarse bracken, and I noticed that in their stony valleys were some stretches of brown, ploughed land, where attempts had been made at cultivation.

I looked to see if there were any signs of civilization remaining on those hills or in the valleys, after the tide of war had ebbed and flowed over them so many times. I did see a group of people outside a rough tent, but all the little white farmsteads (Mussolini's colonisation of the North African littoral) looked tumbledown and deserted.

I continued on the westerly course until I met the road from Martuba, which I followed to Barce, a road which twists between the hills as if a giant's pen had traced their contours. It seemed to me to be a good highway, with a deep foundation and tarmac surface.

Just before reaching Barce, I could see away to the north what looked like numerous large beehives in well-arranged lines. Nearer view revealed them as farm buildings, each with an equal area of land around it.

Barce itself was a very attractive-looking small town, which looked as if it had been transplanted *en bloc* from the Italian countryside. I think every one of us who saw it for the first time that day was attracted by it, so unusual were its buildings in style and colour. And seeing Benghazi a few minutes later – a white town standing out to sea – made me feel then (whatever the political background) what a sad error Italy had made in entering the war on the side of the Axis, only to have lost so much territory, into the cultivation of which she seemed to have put a great deal of planned and energetic enterprise.

The six of us who flew to Magrun were each due, as I have said, to make a second trip. But by the time we had all landed there, several of the RSU's training flight had also arrived, although the advance road party had not. This meant that the pilots would all have to be accommodated temporarily. So to ease this problem (and also make matters easier for ourselves) it was decided that six of the training flight pilots should come back to Gazala with us in the Hudson and take up the remaining machines on the next day. We landed at Gazala III in the blaze of a glorious sunset, dropped the six pilots and left immediately for El Adem, which we reached in the early dusk.

The two other NCOs and I managed to get a substantial meal, which they especially welcomed, as they had had a very early breakfast and only a makeshift lunch. After this we decided to take our blankets from one of the stone-floored rooms adjoining a hangar (the roof of which had been reduced by bombing to odd girders, now silhouetted by moonlight, and on whose walls inscriptions in three languages bore witness to many changes in possession) and put them in the Hudson, where we could spend a more comfortable night.

We were just coming out of the hangar when someone shouted 'Fireworks!' – which is exactly what the Tobruk barrage looked like from the south – a lavish but very businesslike Brock's display.

We stood in the open watching the swift orange dashes from the Bofors guns, as their shells wrote the code of death across the night sky; and we could hear the c-r-r-ump, c-r-r-ump of the big naval guns and see the flashes where their shells exploded high up against the clouds. Flares were coming down from some enemy aircraft – one, two, three, dropping in slow succession and burning with a bright light for a long time until they spluttered and petered out like stars falling from the sky.

The moon was now high and full and, because of the moving clouds, seemed to be racing along with her attendant stars. Gradually the barrage diminished, then ceased. We could hear an aircraft, which sounded like a single-engined one and seemed to be above the clouds; then another, a twin-engined one: they seemed to be diving and turning. Then there was a sudden, short tat-tat-tat of machine-gun or cannon fire and an increasing whee-e-e – the whine of something diving at terrific speed.

'Bombs!' yelled 'Jumbo' Tanner.

We threw ourselves down on the stony ground. There were sparks and four quick explosions somewhere on the aerodrome, and we looked up just in time to see an aircraft at about 200 feet, going hell-for-leather out towards the sea. Then away to the right, black against the clouds, the clear silhouette of a Beaufighter climbing away out of its pursuing dive.

This was the first time I had seen any 'action' at close quarters in the war, apart from the hit-and-run Ju88s at Paignton. The enemy aircraft (which we think was a Ju87 single-engined dive bomber) seemed to have jettisoned its bombs in order to escape the pursuing Beaufighter. Fortunately there seemed to be only one casualty – 'Jumbo' Tanner, who cut his thumbs open when he dived on to the ground. (Poor 'Jumbo', who had so wanted to fly Spitfires. Death's bony finger seemed to have been pointed at him, for a short time after this episode he killed himself at Martuba when making a forced landing in a Kittyhawk).

We were undisturbed for the rest of that night and took off at 6-15 the next morning for Heliopolis, where we had a wash and a leisurely breakfast before returning to LG 209.

By now, only ten days from the end of December 1942, the 8th Army had reached El Agheila, a turning-point in previous desert campaigns, when the advance had out-run supplies and became a retreat; but this time there was no turning back: the next objective was Tripoli. As the Army pressed westwards, the supply distances became formidable; it was about 650 miles from Cairo to Benghazi. Even in a Kittyhawk on 1st January 1943 it was 3hr 45min flying from LG 209 to Magrun, and there was always the matter of getting back to base (on that occasion, hitching a lift in a US Army Air Corps DC-3 from Benina, just east of Benghazi, to Heliopolis).

When I'd got to Magrun (my third trip there) I hitch-hiked up to Benina, getting there in six lifts, and it was interesting to see the changes that had taken place on the road to Benghazi, even in so short a space of time as a week. The road itself was under repair in places, potholes being filled in; various Army camps had appeared, each having a neat notice on the roadside proclaiming its function; and everywhere there was evidence of clearing-up operations. Near the junction of the Magrun-Benghazi road and that to Benina there was a field half filled with a scrap-heap of Italian aircraft; and in another a well-organised football match was in progress – a sure sign that 8th Army support units were there to stay, at least until the Afrika Korps had been driven out of North Africa.

I was fortunate in getting a lift back from Benina in a US Army Air Corps (as it was known then) DC-3 captained by a Staff Sergeant, with a co-pilot of the same rank, the first American NCO aircrew I had encountered. We took off at about noon and immediately ran into bad weather – rain and low cloud about 500ft above the hilltops, and the first half hour was exceptionally bumpy. It was also a tedious flight, like a slow train journey with many stops, for after calling at El Adem (south of Tobruk) we went on to Gambut, where we landed at three aerodromes in quick succession. They were all close together: one was Gambut Main, another was Gambut Satellite; what the other one was I didn't know.

After leaving Gambut we flew into a thick dust haze, but we climbed above it and came into the clear over the sea. Our next landing was at LG 174, which was south of Alexandria, and we took off from there in the gathering dusk. As it became totally dark we observed with interest Cairo's partial blackout – a thousand bright circles and points of light. It was interesting to experience a night landing at Heliopolis – the first night flying I'd done since No 12 Flying Training School at Grantham in July 1941, when we diced with death in the dark skies around Harlaxton in Lincolnshire in Avro Ansons.

I hadn't yet flown a twin-engined type in the Middle East; all through the first half of January 1943 I was put down for delivery flights in Tomahawks (the earlier version of the Kittyhawk), Harvards and Kittyhawks, yet Geoff Mewies, my exact contemporary and one of my closest pals, was already flying Baltimores and Beaufighters. So I had a moan to Ken Charlton (who had been on the first course at Kemble and was by now a Flight Lieutenant and made out the flying programme), who responded on the 12th by saying, "Right. There's a Blenheim for you." So on the 13th I flew a Blenheim V – otherwise known as a Bisley and the poorest-performance version of the Bristol Blenheim series – from Heliopolis to Abu Sueir. This aircraft (BA137) seemed to be hanging in the air on its propellers, but I remember it with affection because it presaged better things to come.

Much was to change for me from February 1943 – new experiences and new friendships, and I seemed at last to "come of age" as a pilot. I'd always been a slow starter, and had taken 10hr 25min to go solo. As mentioned earlier, my instructor at No 16 EFTS, Flying Officer Ron Chalmers, had been very patient with me. I'm glad I met him again in postwar years and was able to thank him.

Because of the constantly increasing distance between the squadrons and RSUs and the Maintenance Units in the Delta area, No 216 Group decided that No 2 ADU should have a forward detachment, and I was lucky enough to be one of the pilots chosen to be on it. We were to be based at Berca Main, Benghazi, with No 136 MU (AAD – Advanced Aircraft Depot).

8. Benghazi Days

We set off on 10 February 1943, taking our own "taxi" – Anson DG766, flown by Warrant Officer BE Brown. "Tom" Brown was one of the finest pilots I have ever encountered; he was a natural flyer and was also a first-class mechanic. One day, taking off from Berca Main towards the barrage balloons which hung over Benghazi harbour and after a very liquid party in the Mess the night before, he did two upward rolls in a Kittyhawk. On another occasion, when we were flying back Hurricanes to the eventual 2 ADU base (LG 237 – Gebel Hamzi on the Cairo-Alexandria road), his aircraft developed a fault. I can't remember what it was – it may have been a glycol leak; but nothing deterred, Tom landed on one of the LGs around Fuka, put the fault right and took off again.

On this occasion his role was much more prosaic, flying us from LG 209 on the Cairo-Suez road to Berca Main, which took 5 hours and ten minutes, with refuelling stops at Mersa Matruh and El Adem. We were to be there until mid-October, when we moved forward to Castel Benito south of Tripoli, and those days at Berca were to be the most active and rewarding of all those in the Middle East for me. Whoever chose our CO made an inspired choice. Flight Lieutenant F W (Fred) Hosken was a South African, charming and with a quiet sense of humour. He had the prestige of having flown Gladiators with No 80 Squadron in the ill-fated Greek campaign of 1941. Anyone who had done that, operating against hopeless odds, was a hero; and Fred Hosken was a modest one. He had flown up to Berca in one of 2 ADU's Hudsons (the unit's long-range transports) on the 9th, and we were lucky to have him in charge. The Anson would remain with us at Berca Main as the detachment's "taxi." A new and adventurous era was about to begin for a small and hardworking group of pilots, flying westwards to new horizons – Tripoli and beyond.

We had exchanged the sand and tents of a landing ground in Egypt for the former civil/military airport of Benghazi, Berca Main, with its Regia Aeronautica permanent buildings and hangars. Just to the north of it was the wrecked town and harbour, littered with sunken ships and guarded now by barrage balloons. We shared the facilities with No 136 MU, for whom we did test flying when not on delivery trips to Tripoli and into Tunisia and Algeria. On the whole, relations were good between ourselves and the Maintenance Unit NCOs, though there was some "aggro" between one or two of the Sergeants and Flight Sergeants who'd spent their whole careers getting those ranks, and here were young Sergeant/Flight Sergeant Pilots who'd only been in the RAF a few months. However, life was too busy for us to suffer from the jealousy of the "regulars," and for most of the time we were away from the aerodrome on ferry trips, which involved night stops as they got longer. By 14 February Fred Hosken reported to base that we were extremely busy and getting about six hours flying in each day.

On the 3rd, before we flew up to Berca Main with Tom Brown, I'd had my first experience of flying in a Beaufighter – which meant standing on the entry/escape hatch behind the pilot. I hitched a ride with Geoff Mewies from Benina to Got Bersis, where No 89 Sqn (whom we knew when they were at Abu Sueir) were then based. I came back to Benina with Flying Officer K W T Pugh, who was doing a night-flying test, and I shall never forget his Rate 6 steep turn around the airfield, standing the aircraft on its wing tip, so that I was pulled downwards by the force of gravity. I was soon to have the opportunity of getting to know the Beaufighter – an aircraft which I loved flying.

Geoff and I shared a room in the Berca Main buildings, which were daubed with Fascist slogans. The accommodation was sparse but it was better than tents. My other close pal, Bob Smart, was also on the detachment; the other pilots, in addition to Tom Brown, were "Deb" Debenham, a New Zealander; "Tich" Fennessey, an Australian; "Mac" McLoughlin, a Canadian; and "Tommy" Thompson. Sadly, Bob and Tommy didn't survive; they lost their lives in 1944. But for that time at Berca Main we were a group of very fit young fellows; when not flying we played volley ball or went swimming on the nearby seashore. I hadn't been able to swim at Manchester Grammar School because of ear trouble, but I soon learned in the rock pools and warm water of the Mediterranean.

Berca Main, a pear-shaped grass airfield with its wider end on the north side where the hangars and buildings were, was a delightful change from all the desert landing grounds. To the north-east was Benina and to the south three other Berca aerodromes, occupied by USAAF B-24 Liberators in pink desert camouflage practising for the major attack on the Ploesti oilfields in Romania which took place on 1 August, and by a Wing of torpedo carrying Beaufighters based there for operations against Axis shipping in the Mediterranean.

We got to know the area well, test flying for No 136 MU and firing aircraft guns at semi-submerged wrecks in Benghazi harbour. During February I flew Kittyhawks and Warhawks to Darragh landing ground, which was beyond Marble Arch, Mussolini's vainglorious white triumphal arch which straddles the road between Benghazi and Tripoli, at the bottom of the Gulf of Sirte. If ever any monument could remind you of Shelley's sonnet *Ozymandias* ('I met a traveller from an antique land'), this was it for:

Round the decay
Of that colossal wreck, boundless and bare
The lone and level sands stretch far away.

Not that Mussolini's Marble Arch was a wreck: it was quite sound, white and shining, but it was a colossal anomaly, rendered meaningless with the collapse of the Fascist Empire. On the north side of the road was the landing ground, and I didn't realise at the time what a price the Afrika Korps had made the 8th Army pay for its capture. Before No 239 Wing of Kittyhawk squadrons could move in there, 20 sappers were killed clearing mines from the access roads and approaches. Initially, squadron ground personnel had to be airlifted in by Hudsons of No 249 Wing, which supported the Desert Air Force throughout the final North African campaign.

One of its squadrons was No 117, one of whose captains, Billy Higham, I met at Marble Arch and who became a lifelong friend. He later joined No 2 ADU and flew the Hudsons which, with the Ansons, formed our "airline" for retrieving pilots from their ferry sorties. Occasionally, however, we had to get back by whatever means were available – however unconventional.

The "unconventional means" of getting back happened to me in our first month at Berca Main, as did several other untoward incidents, two of them pleasant and two of them not so pleasant.

On a beautiful night, with a clear moon and stars and some high cloud, we stood in a slit trench below a high wall, in the garden outside our quarters, watching the terrific Benghazi ack-ack barrage. We could see shells which seemed to clear the hangar roof by inches, and heavy rocket-like ordnance which burst very high up in stars of hot steel. No doubt the Luftwaffe was mounting a nuisance raid from Crete; if so, they got as good as they gave.

I was due to fly a Kittyhawk the following morning to Darragh, beyond Marble Arch, and after take-off did a low circuit over the hangars before setting course along the coastal road.

I then noticed oil streaming back along the fuselage, and the next moment a black, lava-like liquid rapidly spreading over the floor of the cockpit. I turned back towards the airfield, and when I wound back the hood for landing a filmy black spray blew up, obscuring the instrument panel. All this took only a few minutes; the cause was the filler cap on the oil tank being only half on, for which piece of negligence a fitter was put on a charge. My shorts and stockings had to be cleaned up with petrol (not very successfully) and I took off again at half-past one, reaching Marble Arch in an hour. But because the Anson (which Geoff Mewies was flying) was due to leave Darragh at two o'clock, and it would take me an hour and a half to get there, I decided to spend the night in the transit camp – tents pitched on the sand dunes, within sound of the perpetual roaring of the sea breaking on the shore. Geoff picked me up at Darragh but we had to spend a second night at Marble Arch, because it was discovered that the Anson had no navigation lights and its accumulator would only support the landing light momentarily. Poor DG766, the detachment's "taxi," also suffered the indignity of an airman's foot through her mainplane – a mishap rectified temporarily for the flight back to Berca Main.

It took an hour and a quarter by Anson from Marble Arch to Benghazi, following the coastline of the Gulf of Sirte and, after landing at Berca Main, we found that there were about five aircraft to be tested – which it was decided should be 'done' before lunch. Fred Hosken, our admirable and charming CO, asked me if I would like to 'do' a Spitfire. Of course, I didn't say no, and had an exhilarating half-hour.

Flying this famous fighter (a Mark V, ER543) from a grass airfield seemed just right. Having hitherto flown Hurricanes and Kittyhawks, and heavy twins like the Anson and Blenheim, I found it delightfully light and responsive – a graceful thoroughbred. I stooged around the local Cyrenaican sky with a new-found sense of freedom, and at low level banged off its cannons against an old barge half sunk down the coast about twelve miles from Benghazi; then I slipped back into the Berca Main circuit and eased the Spitfire on to the grass with light touches of its sensitive elevators, and a highly satisfied feeling in the cockpit. Of course, since 1938 hundreds of RAF pilots had trained on Spitfires and fought in them, and it was now February 1943; but I think that everyone flying one for the first time got a particular thrill from the experience: I suppose that there has never been a more graceful warplane designed and built.

From the sublime to the mundane, that afternoon Geoff Mewies and I flew down with Fred Hosken in a Messerschmitt Me 108 Taifun, a single-engined four-seater communications aircraft left behind by the Luftwaffe when the Afrika Korps retreated, to Berca III – one of a clutch of landing grounds to the south of Benghazi. A Kittyhawk and a Hurricane were to be picked up there: Geoff was lucky and took the former; I was unlucky because the Hurricane was unserviceable. Fred Hosken must have gone straight back to Berca Main after dropping us off, so I had to return there by gharry, which took much longer than the ten minutes in the Me 108. But I didn't mind: I was still enjoying the afterglow of my Spitfire experience; I had the witty company of our splendid Scots MT driver, Jock (who I think had brought the gharry all the way up from Cairo as the detachment's transport); and I had the early expectation of meeting a school friend from Manchester days, Bill Alban, who happened to be serving in the Benghazi area as a wireless operator with No 247 Wing and who I hadn't seen since about April 1940 – a long time in those wartime years, when so many unimaginable things happened to all of us, things which no one could ever have predicted.

As Bill was 'on watch' in the signals cabin of No 247 Wing our first meeting consisted of a brief word now and then, so I suggested that we should meet again at 7-30 that evening on the Tripoli road. It took me an hour and a half to walk to our rendezvous – under a windy, moonlit sky – but it was well worth it. Getting there took far longer than I had expected and Bill showed faithfulness indeed; he must have been waiting for an hour. Then he kindly shortened my journey back by walking with me towards Benghazi, while we told one another of our experiences since we last met.

Apart from the uniform (KD shirt and shorts) and a moustache he had acquired, he was still the same charming fellow I had known in the 1930s, with a commanding presence and great gifts as an actor. After studying medicine for a year at Leeds University and hating it, he gave up all thoughts of becoming a doctor and joined a local repertory company, which failed early in 1939; so, with war imminent, he pre-empted a call-up by training at the

School of Wireless Telegraphy in Newcastle as a radio operator for the Merchant Navy, passing out with top marks. But then war came and he was called up; the RAF was suffering from an acute shortage of radio operators; so Bill became an AC2 and was posted to the Middle East: hence our meeting on that windswept road near Benghazi – a welcome encounter indeed. I didn't see him again until long after the war; by that time he'd gone to Cambridge to read English and taken up schoolmastering, becoming "Mr Chips" at Hurstpierpoint College, with acting as his second great enthusiasm – at school and with local amateur dramatic companies.

Word must have got back that we'd met, because a few months later I had a letter from Bill's cousin Audrey, an attractive, vivacious, dark-haired girl with whom I'd been very much in love during my school and university days. Then, after a visit with my sister to Audrey's home in Whitley Bay in early 1940, something went wrong and she peremptorily returned the gifts I'd given her. In her letter she referred to herself as 'a stranger', then said 'I'm not really. You once knew me a LONG time ago – remember?' Of course I did: how could I forget? I read her letter countless times – so many times that I came to know its phrases by heart. But I never replied to it: the world had changed so much since those idyllic pre-war days. Nor did I have a girl friend during my RAF years. In the Western Desert, and later constantly on the move in Transport Command, there were few opportunities for meeting girls;

and subconsciously, I suppose, I was always looking for another Audrey.

The day I met Bill, I'd been exhilarating in the Spitfire's aerodynamics over the green countryside around Benghazi. Four days later I was brought down to earth with a bump – literally. I'd been tasked with delivering a Mk I Kittyhawk (ET957) and landed at Marble Arch to refuel. I took off from there and was flying at fairly low level (about 1,500ft, I suppose) when, at about 22 miles west of Sultan at the bottom of the Gulf of Sirte, the engine stopped. (It was known that when the cylinder blocks in the Allison engines were re-bored, there was the possibility of metal fatigue: this is probably what caused mine to seize up). I had no room for manoeuvre, no height to play with; my only option was to land straight ahead. Fortunately this Kittyhawk didn't have an underslung overload fuel tank. Fortunately too the ground was covered in some sort of bracken, which cushioned the impact. I held off as long as I could to kill the speed, but there was the inevitable crunching sound of metal being scraped and fractured. I switched off the ignition and fuel; I'd already wound back the cockpit hood, so I unlocked the Sutton harness and was out in a flash. But there was no fire; only a sudden, complete silence. After a few minutes' contemplation of the wrecked Kittyhawk I slung my parachute over my left shoulder and trudged over the uneven ground towards the coastal road. I had to get back to Berca Main, and the only way was to hitch-hike.

The first vehicle which came along was, believe it or not, a slow-moving tank transporter whose driver informed me that he "didn't think he'd get back to Marble Arch that night" (I'd been flying for twenty minutes). Something faster was needed: there was plenty of MT on that highway supplying the 8th Army, and I got a lift soon, but the day was far spent by the time I reached Marble Arch, and it was the following morning when I got a ride to Benina in a Hudson of No 216 Sqn. But despite my abortive Kittyhawk flight, all was not lost that day; for at Marble Arch (as I mentioned) I met Billy Higham, one of the pilots of No 117 Sqn – which, with the other three transport squadrons (216, 267 and 173) carried up supplies for the Desert Air Force throughout the campaign, who became a lifelong friend. In those circumstances true friendships were formed: one didn't know a chap's social status, political or religious views; one liked him for what he was – especially in the free and easy, non-hierarchical atmosphere of the desert.

By now the 8th Army (which entered Tripoli on 23 January) had on 4 February crossed the frontier into Tunisia: the campaign was entering its final stage with the Afrika Korps' last stand on the Mareth Line.

Kittyhawks in convoy, refuelling at Ikeja airfield, north of Lagos, Nigeria.

Kittyhawks en route.

Recreational transport.

The author, horse riding for a change.

No. 2 ADU detachment pilots: 'Tom' Brown, 'Deb' Debenham,, 'Titch' Baker and Humphrey Wynn at Berca Main, Benghazi.

Marble Arch ~ Mussolini's vainglorious monument.

Pilot Officer Humphrey Wynn on leave in Palestine, April 1944.

Back at Kilo 40 after delivering Spitfires to Greece, October 1944.
Standing l to r: F/O Hunter, F/Lt Lomas, F/O Tregoning and F/O Warboys.
Kneeling: P/O Wynn and F/Sgt Craig.

No 2 ADU C/O Wing Commander J.H. 'Red' Williams (centre, back row) flanked by Squadron Leader A.B.R. Dow (to his left) and Flt Lt Lew Bevis, with Flt Lt Caldicott and Lt Taudi (a Yugoslav pilot) in front.

The cost of war ~ El Adem Cemetery.

No.2 ADU pilots: the C/O Wing Commander J.H. 'Red' Williams is on
the extreme right with the adjutant, Flt Lt B.J. Edgell on his right.

Terminal building at Elmas, Sardinia, a staging post.

Passengers buffet at RAF Elmas, Sardinia, staging post.
Note the Royal Air Force Transport Command badge on the wall.

Allenby Bridge over the River Jordan.

Aden, midday ~ note the short shadows.
The author with co-pilot Flt Lt R.K. 'Kitty' Groves on the left.

At Lydda en route for the UK via Karachi. From left, Pete Carnochan, Jack Fenton and Johnny House, with Boxer in the foreground.

Dakota refuelling at Sharjah.

A faithful Dakota crew: Warrant Officer Pete Carnochan (signaller),
Warrant Officer Jack Fenton (co-pilot) and Flt Lt Johnny House (navigator).

9. Westward Ho

For the first time, the war which had been waged back and forth across the Western Desert since 1940 had moved out of Libya into Tunisia, and the names of landing-grounds with which we had become all too familiar – like Mersa Matruh, Gambut, El Adem, Magrun and Marble Arch – were being replaced by unfamiliar ones like Misurata, Castel Benito, Sorman, Zuara and Ben Gardane. Castel Benito was an established airfield south of Tripoli, one of Mussolini's show places; but many of the LGs, where the RSUs were located, were only distinguished from the surrounding sand by tents and with oil drums marking a runway and were often difficult to find in dust-storm conditions. This was "seat of the pants" flying, at which we became expert; much depended on personal initiative. We were still based at Berca, but flying further and further westwards.

I was also still flying single-engined types – Hurricanes, Kittyhawks and Spitfires – while my closest pals Geoff Mewies and Bob Smart had progressed on to Bostons, Baltimores and Beaufighters. In his usual blunt Yorkshire way Geoff commented one day that Fred Hosken had it in for me for low flying in the Anson when I was bringing a group of pilots back from Castel Benito to Berca. Whether this was true or not, it was a stupid thing to do and I deserved his censure. However, I made the breakthrough in a quite unexpected and informal way, at the beginning of July – only a week before Operation Husky, the invasion of Sicily, began on the night of the 9th/10th and which was to add a brief new dimension to my flying experience.

On the 4th I flew with Tom Brown in a Baltimore from Berca to Marble Arch, and it happened that there was a Douglas Boston there which had to be flown back to No 136 MU. Well, Tom showed me round the cockpit and off I went, on a 1hr 5 min flight across the Gulf of Sirte. Conversion to a new type was just as casual as that in those days.

The Boston, powered by two Wright Cyclone radial engines and with a tricycle undercarriage, was a delight to fly – whatever its merits or limitations as a light bomber, and the difficulties for the three-man crew in abandoning the aircraft in an emergency. With its high fin and rudder it was inherently stable. On a later occasion, when I had an engine failure owing to a fuel pump packing up, the first I knew of it was an indication on the fuel pressure gauge. On this first occasion I experienced complete hydraulic failure shortly after taking off from Marble Arch.

All battle-worn aircraft being flown back by us for major refurbishment were liable to be faulty; we knew this and took it in our stride. I think that by now I was gaining maturity as a pilot, in the freelance kind of flying we were by then accustomed to do: no emergency ever came as any sort of surprise to us.

As Benghazi and its white twin-domed cathedral hoved into view and I prepared to enter the circuit for landing at

Berca Main, I used the emergency hydraulic hand-pump to lower and lock the undercarriage. Then, once established on a final approach, I pumped the flaps down. When the Boston's main wheels rumbled on to the grass airfield and the nose-wheel came down, I pumped again, to activate the brakes; so we came to a controllable taxiing speed, I parked and switched off the engines: my first flight in a Boston was over.

A few months earlier two SAAF Bostons (the South African Air Force made an outstanding contribution to the Western Desert/Mediterranean air war) had collided on take-off from Berca Main. Their crews had stayed overnight; we had a rowdy party and in the morning we stood outside the hangar to watch them go – in formation, and very close together. Just after they got airborne the starboard engine of the left-hand aircraft seemed to cut, and the torque of its port engine pulled it in towards the leading aircraft. It appeared to get caught in its slipstream; with its nose well up it staggered on for a few seconds, then crashed through the trees on the far boundary, over the road and into the field opposite. A cloud of dust rose up – fortunately there was no smoke. The pilot and air gunner got out safely, but the observer – in the nose of the Boston – was badly injured and died at about two o'clock in the afternoon. As always when such accidents occur, it was a shaking experience to see an aircraft at one moment complete and powerful and the next moment a broken wreck on the ground, with crew casualties – young men complete and strong, then whisked into eternity or maimed for life. Geoff Mewies and I were in sombre mood when we took off in Kittyhawks a few minutes later; but in those days, flying casualties were the daily stuff of our lives.

During May, when in the latter part of the month there was very little work to do, we went down to the beach every afternoon for sun and sea-bathing; we had also acquired a black rubber dinghy with oars, so were able to do some rowing as well. We also watched the B-24s (Liberators) going out in the morning and returning in the afternoon. Sometimes when they were forming up they were shepherded by a P-40, weaving in and out among them like a sheepdog amongst his flock.

These B-24s, in pink or tawny desert camouflage, belonged to the USAAF 9th Bomber Command, which had five bomb groups in the Benghazi area, practising for a low-level daylight attack on the Ploesti oil refineries in Romania. They were based at Lete, Benina, Berka Two and Four and Terria, and replicas of their targets were marked out in the desert south of Benghazi. They flew off into the "bundu" and their aim was to return at very low level and deliver their practice bombs exactly on time. The differences between their training area and the real thing were that, in Libya, there were no fighter and ack-ack defences and no weather or navigational problems.

We were unaware at the time as to what exactly was going on: the B-24s were just another aspect of the continuing air war in the Mediterranean. When the big day came, and 177 B-24s took off at 7 o'clock in the morning of 1 August on Operation Tidal Wave (as it was called), I was away from Berca Main: I had taken a Kittyhawk to Sorman near Tripoli on 31 July, been flown to Castel Benito in a Boston later that day, and had brought a Boston back to 136 MU on the 1st. By that time the oil refineries had been bombed, 54 B-24s had been lost, 440 USAAF aircrew had been killed or were missing, 54 were wounded, 79 interned in Turkey and about 200 known to be prisoners of war[5]. This was a terrible price to pay for an attack which was only partially successful and which only temporarily affected the flow of fuel to Wehrmacht tanks and Luftwaffe aircraft. The flight distance from Benghazi was 2,300 miles, and it is certain that the defenders knew that the B-24s were coming, from prior Intelligence and because they had a Signal Interception Battalion near Athens. Although Ploesti was attacked again, there was no repetition of this low-level raid from the Benghazi area, which was comparable with Bomber Command's costly attacks by Lancasters of Nos 44 and 97 Squadrons on Augsburg in April 1942, a daylight sortie in which nearly half the force (five aircraft out of 12) was lost.

I was away from Berca when the great attack on Ploesti took place: I had flown a Kittyhawk to Sorman, a landing ground west of Tripoli, on the last day of July and got a lift from there to Castel Benito in a Boston flown by Pilot Officer Johnstone. How was I to get back to Berca? Well, I

---

5. We knew nothing of this at the time, and I am indebted for these details to two books, Ploesti: The Great Ground-Air Battle of 1 August 1942 by James Dugan and Carroll Stewart (Jonathan Cape, 1963) and Low Level Mission by Leon Wolff (Longmans, Green and Co, 1958).

flew a Boston, via Marble Arch, on 1 August. By the time I got back, Operation Tidal Wave was over: many brave fellows had lost their lives or become PoW.

Ironically, only a few miles from the B-24 airfields, our small part in the 1939-45 air war continued in its steady way: I did over 28 hours' flying that month, in Spitfires, Kittyhawks and Bostons, and was getting to know the littoral of Tripolitania like the back of my hand. But big changes, and new adventures, were in the offing.

Early in September our well-liked CO, Fred Hosken, was posted back to the Union of South Africa, tour-expired: he left a very friendly memory behind, and I had the good luck to meet him once more, in post-war years, at the RAF Club in London when we had a hastily-arranged rendezvous with 'Red' Williams. When he took his leave of the Berca detachment, which he had commanded with charm and distinction, Fred earmarked a Boston to fly himself back to the Delta after handing-over on the 5th. As luck would have it he only got as far as El Adem, where the Boston went U/S (unserviceable) so he had to continue his journey as a passenger. At the RAF Club he told us of another slice of bad luck: a new road was to be driven through his grounds, cutting them in two. I don't know what the outcome of that was.

Fred's successor as our CO was Flight Lieutenant Bob Kings, a handsome ex-Battle of Britain pilot who apparently held the record for the number of times he baled-out during that conflict. We also acquired a new Adjutant, Flying Officer 'Rocky' Stone, and these two developed a close confidence which somehow didn't extend to the NCO pilots: the rapport we had enjoyed with Fred Hosken was missing. This was especially marked after the detachment moved forward to Castel Benito, Tripoli, Mussolini's aerial gateway to his African empire, in October. By then the battle scenario had changed: Operation Husky, the Allied invasion of Sicily, had been mounted on 9/10 July from Tunis. Africa was now clear of the Afrika Korps, the Luftwaffe, the Italian 10th Army and the Regia Aeronautica.

Reinforcement of the Allied air and ground forces pressing on from Sicily into Italy was now the order of the day.

Operation Husky and the earlier Operation Torch landings in Algeria to link up with the 8th Army and bring in the Americans for a full-scale assault on Italy – which Churchill had referred to as "the soft under-belly of Europe" – had changed the operational scenario of the Mediterranean war. As far as our aircraft reinforcement role was concerned, new Aircraft Delivery Units were formed – No 3 at Fez in Morocco (later moved to Oujda) to fly aircraft from there to Cairo and on to India, and No 4 at Azizia, south of Tripoli, to reinforce the Desert Air Force (as it was still called) in Italy.

Our own instructions to move to Castel Benito came on 18 October, but in our last month at Berca I had some lively new experiences. On 16 September (my birthday) I had flown a Boston to Sorman, a landing-ground west of Tripoli, near a sensational Roman amphitheatre, when I was "commandeered" by Lt-Col Bill Bryden, CO of No 4 ADU (all the SAAF officers had Army ranks), whom I remembered when he was a convoy leader on the West African Reinforcement Route, to fly another Boston to Sicily; and on this occasion I had a crew – Flight Sergeant Parkinson and Sergeant Wilson. It took an hour and 45 minutes to fly to Pachino, set in the dusty Sicilian olive groves, and from there we were ordered on to Gerbini No 7, where we relinquished the Boston and got a lift back to Pachino in an Anson of No 24 (SAAF) Squadron. There, there was a Boston to be taken back to Egypt, so we climbed aboard for the 35-minute flight to Luqa, Malta.

All seemed to be plain sailing, but then disaster struck. On take-off from Luqa, heading towards a quarry at the end of the main runway, the nose-wheel tyre burst. My immediate reaction was to abort the take-off, so I pulled back the throttles; my second reaction was to safeguard Flight Sergeant Parkinson, who was in the navigator's compartment in the nose: so I pulled back hard on the controls to kill off speed and keep the nose wheel off the ground as long as possible. Eventually, of course, it came down, juddered and collapsed; but apart from being shaken, Parkinson was OK. We had to get a Dakota ride back to Castel Benito on the following day – which was the prelude for me of another new experience: flying a Baltimore for the first time, from Castel Benito to Marble Arch and then to Berca – the twin-engined Martin medium bomber, produced especially for the RAF, which with the Boston had been a staple of the DAF medium-bomber arm in support of the 8th Army. It was powered by two extremely reliable Wright Cyclone radial engines, and I never had any trouble with any one of the type I flew, though the earlier models had a tendency to swing on take-off and we were to witness a landing tragedy, with an inexperienced pilot, at Castel Benito during November 1943.

Built by the American Glenn Martin Co to a British specification, the Baltimore was an unglamorous but sturdy and reliable wartime bomber. The Bristol Beaufighter, which I first flew on 27 November, was an aircraft of great character and fine pedigree; its direct ancestor was the Blenheim, which suffered so severely in 1940-41 operations. Unlike the Blenheim, it had plenty of power – two 1,600 hp Bristol Hercules engines; and the pilot, sitting between them, had a commanding view.

There was no chance of any dual instruction on the Beaufighter: all you could do was stand on the access hatch (which was also the escape hatch) behind the pilot and watch what he did. I'd done this several times, with my friends Geoff Mewies and Bob Smart and with Flying Officer Pugh of 89 Squadron when we were at Berca Main; but when it came to it the opportunity was unexpected: I was to fly one from Castel Benito to the MU at Setif in the Atlas Mountains, via Biskra on the edge of the Sahara – a double incentive, because I was very fond of the girl in reception at the Hotel Transatlantique where we used to night-stop. Since, too, it was a 3hr 35min trip from CB to Biskra I had plenty of time to get the feel of the aircraft – a real thoroughbred, which I loved flying and of which I was to have much greater experience during 1944. Fortunately I had an easy indoctrination, because the short hop to Setif the following morning could not have offered a more marked contrast – from the unending vista of Sahara desert to green, mountainous terrain often plagued by cloud and rain, which could turn the landing-ground into a quagmire.

It was only a couple of days later that we witnessed at close quarters a Baltimore disaster, when one of our young pilots who had just converted to the type came in to land at Castel Benito; flying an all-white machine – the camouflage used by maritime squadrons. He had a passenger, sitting in the observer's position in the nose. The aircraft wheels touched and it bounced into the air, then just hung there: we yelled at the pilot to put on power and kill the impending stall, but he did nothing. For a few seconds the Baltimore barely stayed airborne, then as speed fell off the port wing came down, hit the ground and crumpled; over went the aircraft and exploded in a burst of oily black smoke and flame. The war had claimed two more lives, in an avoidable accident, due to the pilot's inexperience. I learned later that his father was a clergyman, who lived in Tenby, South Wales.

Flying from Castel Benito, once the aerial gateway to Mussolini's vainglorious African empire, had its advantages: the climate was equable, though hot (Azizia, to the south, was one of the hottest places I ever experienced – at 117°F nearly as hot as Wadi Haifa), and the surrounding terrain was flat – fortunately, because on one occasion I had to put down a Hurricane on a road. Flying from Berca Main, Benghazi, I encountered a very strong headwind and knew I wasn't going to "make it" to CB. I got a message through about some emergency fuel, and think I slept in the cockpit till the bowser came and I could take off. Somehow, things like that were taken in one's stride.

There were no problems about Castel Benito as a base: it had one long south-north runway and a shorter east-west one; but the tight-knit companionship we enjoyed at Berca Main had gone, partly because Bob Kings was a much more aloof CO than Bunny Hosken and partly because some of the "old hands" like that brilliant pilot Tom Brown had been posted back to the UK.

The advantages of flying from there were that we came to know more of Tripolitania, and of Tunisia and Algeria. Just west of Tripoli were the spectacular Roman ruins at Sorman, a vivid reminder that the North African coast was once part of the Roman Empire; and Tunis, where the last of the Afrika Korps were driven in to the sea, was once Carthage, once the capital of the Carthaginian Empire which was Rome's bitterest enemy ("Carthago delenda est" – "Carthage must be destroyed," thundered Cato in the Roman Senate).

My first sight of Maison Blanche, the big airfield outside Algiers which was the aerial gateway for forces involved in the invasions of Sicily and Italy, came when I flew a Spitfire there from Castel Benito. First up to El Aouina, which was the main airfield for Tunis, via Ben Gardane and Sorman; then westwards to Bone and then to Maison Blanche – five hours 55 minutes' flying time all told. Coming back in a Dakota took 5 hours and 20 minutes – an odd discrepancy, but I think his route was more direct; mine had to be flown in short hops.

In our last month at Castel Benito (November 1943) we regularly flew Baltimores and Beaufighters to the MU at Setif in the Atlas Mountains, night-stopping at Biskra, and on one of these trips I encountered the AOC-in-C again.

Like that meeting with him outside Air Headquarters in Cairo in November 1941, this encounter with Sir Arthur Tedder almost exactly two years later was again an accidental one. He was staying at the Hotel Transatlantique in Biskra, where we night-stopped, on a brief second honeymoon. He had married Lady 'Toppy' Black, who had started the Malcolm Clubs for Servicemen in North Africa, after he had been tragically widowed in January 1943. His first wife was killed when the aircraft in which she was flying back to Cairo from Benina hit the hills surrounding Heliopolis when attempting to land in a sandstorm.

We were making for the bar for a drink before dinner when one of the chaps who had just got inside the door spotted a shoulder with a broad air rank stripe and three more stripes, and hurriedly backed out. But Tedder was too quick for him, seized him by the arm and pulled him in, saying: "No, come on in, chaps; this is where you want to be."

This was typical of Tedder: he hated formality and never "pulled rank;" he had a way of getting on with people, whether they were airmen or NCO pilots like ourselves.

Our days in that part of North Africa were now numbered. During 1943, No 2 ADU pilots delivered 5,716 aircraft locally – that is, within short range of its LG237 (Gebel Hamzi) base on the Cairo-Alexandria road – and 6,223 to the Western Desert, North Africa and elsewhere, a total of 11,939 delivery flights. On 13 December the AOC No 216 Group, Air Commodore Whitney Straight, inspected the detachment at Castel Benito and no doubt told Bob Kings during his visit that it was to be moved back to base. Its commitments would be fulfilled by No 3 ADU at Fez, Morocco, moving aircraft from Casablanca to Cairo; and by No 4 ADU at Azizia south of Tripoli, which would reinforce the squadrons in Sicily and Italy.

So, on 7 January 1944, the detachment received instructions to return to base, and by the 13th the move was completed. For me, this was a new era, and the New Year turned out to be a successful and interesting one in many different ways – both in the air and on the ground. My desert experience had prepared me for fresh challenges.

10. A year of New Adventures

Three black tarmac runways and a perimeter track alongside the black tarmac military road from Mena to El Alamein, set in the unending yellow Egyptian sand to the west of the Nile Delta; two brick buildings – the Officers' and NCOs' Messes – and rows of white tents: this was LG (landing ground) 237, otherwise known as Gebel Hamzi, the base of No 2 Aircraft Delivery Unit, where I was to live and fly during 1944 – the year when the tide of the war turned for the Allies with the landings in Normandy on 6 June, Operation Overlord.

Our detachment at Castel Benito had been wound up by 13 January, but I was to make one more trip to Maison Blanche, and the return Algiers-Cairo flight seemed to me to sum up all those months in the Western Desert and familiarity with the North African coastline to Tunis and beyond.

I had been back at LG237 about two weeks when I was sent off to collect a Baltimore from No 107 MU at Kasfareet on the shore of the Great Bitter Lake and fly it to Setif, the MU in the Atlas Mountains south-east of Algiers, via our familiar landing-grounds – Mersa Matruh, El Adem, Marble Arch, Castel Benito and Biskra. I took a passenger from there to Setif, and Flight Sergeant de Courcy flew me to Maison Blanche in a Wellington. It was from there that I had that unforgettable Beaufighter flight –

some 1700 miles back to Cairo in an aircraft which above all others I enjoyed flying, for its splendid all-round visibility from the cockpit and two magnificent 1,600 hp Hercules engines whirling away almost effortlessly on either side. No wonder the Japanese, who were subjected to its awesome firepower, called the aircraft "whispering death." My flight was purely peaceful.

I had a passenger, Flight Lieutenant Camden, who wanted to get to Cairo, and this was the quickest means possible; but we didn't have an auspicious start. Maison Blanche was choc-a-bloc with US Army Air Corps C-54s, which seemed to arrive in an unending stream. I waited by the side of the runway for a take-off clearance, but it never came, and the Hercules didn't take kindly to ground running: the cylinder head temperatures rose inexorably. Eventually I had to go; I could wait no longer. I can still hear the controller shouting "Clear the runway, fighter;" but it was now or never: throttles hard forward, check for swing, and we were off.

This was the only time I flew from Algiers to Cairo, and I remember having a sense of exhilaration about the flight. It was a kind of signing-off after 12 months' continuous flying during 1943 along the North African littoral – from the Western Desert into Cyrenaica, Tripolitania, Tunisia and Algeria, historic terrain along the blue Mediterranean that I had come to know almost like the back of my hand, and over which I flew with the confidence of youth and experience.

Once I got Beaufighter ND283 airborne from Maison Blanche this splendid aircraft gave us a dream flight, with – for me – a strong sense of déjà vu, a feeling that the part of the world I was looking down on I would never see again[6]. It took three hours to reach Tripoli (Castel Benito), and on the following day two hours 20 minutes to Benina, with its memories (for me) of Benghazi days; then a final two hours 50 minutes to Cairo West, where I said farewell to Flight Lieutenant Camden, who could not have had a smoother or a swifter lift to wherever he was going – on leave or posting.

Cairo West (LG224) was only a few miles "down the road" from Gebel Hamzi (LG237), now my home base with about a hundred other pilots and a sprinkling of navigators and signallers who formed the aircrew element of No 2 Aircraft Delivery Unit, plus groundcrew who serviced its communications flight, and administrative, stores and medical staff. The Unit occupied the whole of the LG237 airfield and had as its neighbour No 135 MU, a maintenance unit/aircraft stores park whose huge stock of aircraft – some of which we test-flew or delivered from time to time – were parked out in the open in unending rows in the desert sands, most of them destined never to fly again and doubtless the cause of many post-war headaches as to their disposal.

No 2 ADU was a well-run unit, with a strong CO (Wg Cdr J.H. "Red" Williams) and a very efficient Adjutant (Flt

---

6. I was in fact to see it again in 1945, and in an El Adem-based exercise in October 1964, which I went on as my RAFVR annual training.

Lt Brian Edgell, an Australian). Its operational objective was to deliver aircraft anywhere in the Mediterranean area, eastwards to India and southwards to South Africa.[7]

Each night a programme of aircraft movements would be 'phoned through from No.216 Group and taken down by the indispensable LAC Coombes. Pilots would walk to the Ops Room in the evening to find out what they were to do on the following day – what type of aircraft they were to fly, where they would pick it up and where they were to take it.

Backing-up these aircraft movements was a Communications Flight, in effect a small airline equipped with Lockheed Hudsons for the longer-range trips and Avro Ansons for shorter ones. This Flight was maintained by an extremely efficient team of fitters and riggers, headed by the Engineering Officer, Flt Lt Dick Abbott, and his senior NCO, Flt Sgt Wilf Burnett. I can't remember one of these transport aircraft ever having let us down.

"Red" Williams not only had the responsibility for all the aircrew under his command; he was also responsible for the security of LG237 Gebel Hamzi, which was vulnerable to incursions by fellahin from villages in the Delta area – only a few miles eastwards. They were silent and extremely skilful thieves who could penetrate the wire security fence, take a man's wallet from under him as he slept in his tent or remove the tyres from a vehicle, then disappear as

---

7. On 19 February Sgts John Tarling, 'Pop' Meggs and 'Judder' Deighton returned to base after delivering Miles Martinet target-towing aircraft from Gibraltar to Coimbatore, southern India, a flight of more than 7,000 miles – the longest undertaken by No 2 ADU.

unobtrusively as they came. "Red's" trademark was a Ford estate car in desert camouflage: if we saw it tearing round the perimeter track, closely followed by a cloud of sand, we knew there was trouble of some kind.

But there was one exception to the thieving fellahin: Quooys Qetir (as we all knew him), familiar because of his gnarled brown face and the piece of sacking he wore as he weaved his way cheerfully around picking up "unconsidered trifles," trudged goodness knows how many miles every day to Gebel Hamzi and was accepted as an errant philosopher, an accepted, mobile part of the desert landscape.

Those of us who lived in the white tents which Quooys poked around with his stick were fit young men who took everything in their stride, whatever the next day might bring, whether a "local" trip from Cairo West to Gebel Hamzi (20 minutes) or a long-range one, which involved being picked-up by one of the Hudsons or making one's own way back.

On 20 February I flew a Vickers Wellington for the first time, from Heliopolis to Ein Shemer in Palestine, with two passengers – neither of them aware of my inexperience. When they got out one of them said to me "How many hours have you got on these, sir?" (I'd just been commissioned and rejoiced in the lowest of the low, as commissioned ranks go, a brand-new Pilot Officer). Fortunately my landing had been smooth – the Wellington, like the Anson, was a very forgiving aircraft – so I confessed that I had never flown one before. By that stage of flying experience one's confidence was high.

At the beginning of 1944, after much thought about it and coming to the conclusion that my relations with my friends would not be affected, I applied for a commission. When the paperwork came through, "Red" Williams grilled me for half-an-hour in his office, with my application form on the desk in front of him. He asked whether I thought I would make a good officer, and whether I'd make as good a one as the average officer of those days.

Going through the form, he asked me to amplify some of my written statements, then having asked why I joined the Air Force he proceeded to more general questions like 'When do you think this war will end?' His final one was: 'Supposing the Armistice had been signed, flying had been stopped to save fuel and you had under your command (say) 100 men, what sort of things would you organise to occupy their time?' My answers seemed to satisfy him and he concluded the interview with 'Well, I'll let you know, Flight'. I saluted and left, not knowing whether the interview had been successful or not, but it seemed to be a fair one[8].

That was on 30 January, and I had my answer on 1 March when I was interviewed at Cairo West by the station commander, Group Captain J W C Simpson DFC and Bar, a handsome ex-Battle of Britain pilot (No 43 Sqn). His questions were few and quick: 'What were you doing before you joined up?' 'How long have you been on 2 ADU and where have you been ferrying?' 'What would you do if you

---

8. On 16 March "Red" was promoted to Wing Commander.

were a Welfare Officer on an isolated unit in the desert?' Of my answer to this last question he said: 'That's good. The AOC is very keen on the welfare of the men. When you become an officer that's a thing you want to look out for. Well, I'll be glad to…'.

I don't know whether he finished this last sentence or not; I saluted and went out as he signed my form. By the time I was back in the Orderly Room he was in his car and halfway down the road. The sequel was a brief entry in the No 2 ADU ORB (Operations Record Book) for 15 April which said: '173003 P/O Wynn commences duty as an officer'. This was the prelude to my last, productive and most interesting eight months' flying in the Middle East.

One of the advantages of being in the Officers' Mess was that we played volley ball on afternoons when we were not flying. One of the ablest exponents was Flying Officer Ali Sabri, one of the half-dozen Egyptian Air Force officers who were seconded to No 2 ADU, and probably the most likeable. He took great pride in being fit and was a handsome fellow. We were not to know then that our wartime association with him was to cause us some embarrassment – to say the least – in post-war years.[9]

_____

9. This happened when we made a reunion trip to Cairo in October 1966 and endeavoured to contact Ali Sabri beforehand, to renew acquaintance with him and smooth our path to visit our "old haunts" like LG237. Unfortunately he had fallen out of favour with Colonel Nasser and we were regarded with some suspicion when we went to visit Gebel Hamzi – still the same old sand and the same old water tower – and we were followed out from Cairo by Egyptian security forces. How were we to know that next year (1967) the Israeli Air Force would make a devastating attack on neighbouring Cairo West? We were

The other change – apart from quite different company in the Mess – was "moving house," to a tent in the officers' lines which I shared with Flt Lt B J ("Doc") Watson, a quietly spoken pilot with a background in the aviation industry. Before the war he had been with Blackburn Aircraft at Brough in East Yorkshire – a company to which he returned after demobilisation. He had the distinction of flying with Lt-Cdr Derek Whitehead, Blackburn's chief test pilot, as flight test observer on the maiden flight of the NA.39 – which became the Buccaneer – on 30 April 1958.

I must add that being commissioned didn't affect any of my friendships on No 2 ADU: we were all pilots – that was what mattered, and the distinction between ranks was blurred in the Western Desert area. I got measured for a "best blue" uniform in Cairo, and had my photograph taken "for the record," but that's all; I increased my flying experience, around the Mediterranean area and to India, flew a few more types, like the Wellington and B-24 Liberator, and was given new commitments – like leading a convoy of Spitfires to Greece and becoming a Beaufighter demonstrator.

I know that, by 1944, hundreds of volunteer aircrew had been commissioned – there was no distinction in that – and hundreds of wartime-trained pilots had taken part in hazardous operations over Europe, in the Western Desert and Italy and the Far East, wining well-deserved DFCs and DSOs: my contribution to the war had been humdrum and

---

no doubt regarded with suspicion, for these were sensitive Egyptian military areas, but our motives were those of genuine ex-service "sightseers".

unheroic. But flying in the 1939-45 air war was multi-faceted, and in the case of ferry pilots in the Middle East, very much a matter of personal initiative: from one day to the next you never knew what type of aircraft you were to fly, or where. The experiences I had in 1944 were unique; nothing daunted me, and I don't think there has ever been anything like the kind of flying we did, which was decidedly informal. If you were designated to fly a new type, you "found out about it" from someone experienced on it, who showed you "the knobs and tits." Only in the case of the B-24 Liberator did I have anything like a formal "conversion" – at Cairo West, as I shall recount. Most operational aircraft were not designed for dual tuition: you were "by yourself" from the word "go." In the Beaufighter you stood behind the pilot and watched what went on, and I found myself giving these demonstrations. I always regret that I never flew a de Havilland Mosquito, nor a Martin Marauder, which was regarded as a "hot ship" because of its high (for those days) landing speed. Poor Frank Kouba, one of my highly esteemed fellow pilots, took one off from Kasfareet on the Bitter Lake (No 107 MU) one day, to realise when he got airborne that he had no airspeed indicator reading – the ASI being one of the most critical instruments on the blind flying panel. Fortunately, Frank "kept his cool," managed to get the "feel" of the aircraft and its power settings and nursed it round to a safe – but what must have been rather a "scary" – landing. Even with new – or reconditioned – aircraft coming out of a Maintenance Unit like that one (and No 107 MU had a very good reputation), and even when they had been test-flown, things could go wrong: aircraft are very complicated pieces of machinery.

But despite such mechanical uncertainties, as far as flying was concerned we had untrammelled use of the skies – a wonderful liberty.

There was always a feeling of uncertainty about our visits to the Ops Room in the evening to find out what we were flying, and where, on the following day. It might be a short trip, within the Delta area, and we would be back at Gebel Hamzi by mid-morning; or we might be away for days. There were further uncertainties about the aircraft, even though it had been prepared by one of the MUs, and the weather if a long trip was involved.

On 16 March I was detailed to fly a Baltimore from Gebel Hamzi to Berca I, our old stamping-ground from detachment days. I made a refuelling stop at El Adem, then when I was en route from there to Berca the hydraulics failed. I debated mentally what to do, but decided that as I was going to an MU (No 136) it was best to press on; there was no point in returning to El Adem. Also, if I had to do a belly landing, the grass airfield at Berca would be a receptive surface.

When I got there I tried every possible emergency means of lowering the undercarriage, but to no avail; I also flew around as long as possible to use up fuel. When I eventually slid on to the grass in a belly landing I'd been airborne all told for five hours and 10 minutes. By contrast, when I flew a Hurricane back from Berca to Helwan on the following day it took me three hours, 45 minutes.

Later that month I had an exhilarating trip to Nicosia in a Beaufighter – my first visit to the beautiful island of Cyprus, long before the post-war days of package holidays. There it was, laid out before me, as I approached from the coast of the Lebanon. I was leading a small convoy of three Beaufighters bound for No 166 MU; the others were flown by Geoff Soutar and "Shorty" Laird (a New Zealand sheep farmer in civil life) and the weather was perfect, with visibility more than 50 miles.

Flying at 5,000ft, just before reaching Tel Aviv we could clearly see the snow-covered mountain range north of the Sea of Galilee, the Jebel ech Cheikh. After passing Haifa we reduced height to 3,000ft and over Saida (once the famed Phoenician port of Sidon) turned on to course for Nicosia. The weather was beautifully calm and the visibility still excellent: when still over 50 miles away we began to see the mountains of Cyprus outlined against the sky. We landed at Nicosia – a good aerodrome with three concrete runways – after 2hr 35min flying and were given a quite effusive welcome, mainly because it didn't appear to be an everyday occurrence to receive aircraft at the MU.

How were we to get back to Gebel Hamzi? We were told that there was a Hurricane I to go to the MU at Helwan, and as Geoff and Shorty Laird were not qualified to fly single-engined types it was arranged that I would fly it back, while they booked passages on a transport aircraft in the morning. When all this booking-in, etc, had been completed we had a leisurely meal in the Sergeants' Mess then hitched a lift into Nicosia, where we found accommodation for the night at the YMCA, a pleasant building with wide, airy rooms upstairs and a balcony overlooking what was more or less the centre of the town, which we sauntered out to have a look at after a cup of tea in the restaurant downstairs.

We noticed the predominance of English cars – Morris Oxfords, Vauxhalls and Austins among them – and the policemen, of whom there seemed to be a large number, wearing familiar uniforms but with flat-topped hats and "CP" on their shoulders.

The town seemed to have two distinct parts – one in which there was some pleasant greenery, a park and some well-built houses; the other which seemed to be much older, consisting of narrow, winding streets thronged with small shops and cafes, amongst which I noticed one called the Othello Bar.

I'd brought a copy of Shakespeare's *Othello* with me, thinking it would be interesting to read amidst the local colour of the island where the drama's tragedy occurs; but far from having time for reading, I found myself during the evening an actor in a real-life comedy. The scene was one of the Nicosia cabarets, the characters, we three and a little girl of Turkish origin; the script was best left unrecorded. Suffice to say that I paid for far too many tots of Muscat (at 2s a time) but didn't break my non-smoking, non-drinking Lenten resolution, though enjoyed a hilarious evening, which only ended when we got back to the YMCA at 11-30 and enjoyed a good night's rest.

In the morning we had a cup of tea in bed and after breakfast (which with our night's accommodation cost us 4s each) took a taxi to the aerodrome, costing 6s between us. I watched the Lockheed Lodestar, with Geoff and Shorty on board, take off at 9 o'clock and was airborne myself ten minutes later. I didn't much fancy the sea crossing, but the faith I'd always had in Rolls-Royce Merlins was unshaken. After a short stop at Lydda in Palestine for refuelling I landed at Helwan at 1 o'clock, and after lunch flew a Baltimore to Gebel Hamzi with two passengers – completing a very satisfying "round trip."

At the end of March 1944 I achieved 1,000 hours' flying, on 15 different types, after exactly three years as a pilot. Many more experiences, and types of aircraft, were to come.

I felt I had only just "graduated" – 1944 was to prove an exceptional year. Meanwhile, there were occasional mundane tasks.

All the twin-engined pilots on No 2 ADU were expected to take a turn in flying the "taxi" Anson – going round the MUs in the Delta area where aircraft were ready to be flown to RSUs or squadrons, dropping off or picking up pilots as required. Avro Ansons, whose original wartime role was maritime reconnaissance in Coastal Command, around the shores of the UK, were used for short-range taxi duties and Lockheed Hudsons for the longer ones. No 2 ADU had a small airline of Ansons and Hudsons, looked after by our

Engineering Officer, Flt Lt Dick ("Bud") Abbott, and his Senior NCO, Flt Sgt Wilf Burnett. I can't remember one of their aircraft ever having let us down, though the Ansons – the epitome of reliability with their Armstrong Siddeley Cheetah radial engines – were decidedly elderly. What they carried on occasion in terms of bodies (plus parachutes) would have driven a loadmaster scatty. I've known one of our "Annies" return to Gebel Hamzi and about 15 pilots climbed out.

Flying around the Delta area in the Anson, the whole of that fertile area of Egypt was spread out like a map, the fertile green area of the Nile contrasting with the endless desert to the West. On a typical passenger-carrying run, we would fly to Heliopolis – that historic sandy RAF station marked to the east by an escarpment and to the west by blocks of flats, or to Helwan south of Cairo, then to Fayid or Kasfareet or Kabrit on the Great Bitter Lake, Egypt's eastern boundary, then up to Aboukir or Edcu on the Mediterranean coast near Alexandria, then perhaps to Bilbeis on the southern edge of the Delta area, or to Cairo West, which was only a few miles from Gebel Hamzi (it took ten minutes to fly from one to the other), and was being developed as a major staging post for aircraft in transit from the UK to India. I came to know Bilbeis and Cairo West well later that year, when I did a conversion course on to Consolidated B-24 Liberators, which with the Boeing B-17 Flying Fortresses formed the USAAC long-range bombing force.

On 12-14 August I flew a Baltimore to Malta, night-stopping at Castel Benito. When I took off from there on the morning of the 13th and set course for Luqa, the weather was so bad I had to return, completing my flight – and returning to Cairo West by Dakota – on the 14th. Little did I realise what tragic news I would hear when I got back to Gebel Hamzi.

Bob Smart – with Geoff Mewies my closest pal since we came out to the Middle East together in October 1941 – had been killed on the 12th.

He had been awarded the AFM (Air Force Medal) earlier that year in recognition of his outstanding service and was one of the most respected pilots of No 2 ADU. As such, he was detailed to lead a convoy of Hurricanes to South Africa, flying a Baltimore with a navigator/wireless operator crew. When they were about 100 miles south of Malakal in the Sudan, heading for Juba, a dreadful misadventure occurred.

It seems they encountered a severe tropical storm, and Bob must have decided to turn back. I don't know whether the Hurricane pilots were in R/T (radio telephone) contact with the Baltimore, or whether Bob waggled its wings to get them into echelon starboard formation, but a fatal mix-up occurred. As a result, the Baltimore with its crew (Warrant Officer Smart, Pilot Officer E Taylor the navigator and Flight Sergeant F Marlor the wireless operator) and two passengers collided with three of the Hurricanes and fell to earth near a village called Ayod.

As a result of the inaccessibility of the terrain, their bodies and the wreckage of the four aircraft were not located until many weeks later. Geoff and I went to see Bob's parents at King's Langley, Hertfordshire, after the war, and we also saw Midge Hichisson his fiancée – one of the girls we'd met in Chippenham when we were doing our conversion course at Kemble with the Service Ferry Squadron in September 1941. A burial service for the eight victims of this tragic accident was held at Malakal Christian Cemetery on 2 February 1947 – a sad, far-distant reminder of a few of the thousands of RAF casualties during the war years.

Sad thoughts about the fate of Bob and his colleagues were not far from our minds when our CO, Wg Cdr "Red" Williams, himself flew me to Bilbeis in one of the unit's Ansons on 15 August: I had been attached to No 1330 Conversion Unit there to learn how to fly Liberators, squadrons of which were being formed in India for long-range bombing operations against Japanese targets. Their aircraft, ferried from the USA to the Middle East, were to be taken on by No 2 ADU pilots.

I did my first trips at Bilbeis, having carefully studied the Liberator systems and made copious notes on the cockpit drills (in a brown-covered HMSO exercise book which I still have), with Flt Lt Eltringham – days of flying round the airfield circuit, then feathering one of the engines, then doing three-engined landings. After about ten days at Bilbeis my Liberator "education" moved to Cairo West, where I had as an instructor a veteran Polish pilot, Warrant Officer Morawski. I remember he once pulled the throttles back to abort a take-off because the windscreen was misted-over with overnight dew, which I thought would quickly clear; but he was right to be cautious and I was taught a valuable lesson. By 4 September, when my course ended, I was "certified fit to ferry Liberator aircraft" by Flt Lt W F Ellis the Chief Flying Instructor at No 1330 CU.

I did several trips to India, and some shorter-range flying, in Liberators but never counted them as among my favourite aircraft. Their main virtues were the tricycle-undercarriage configuration, which made take-off and landing easy, and their ever-reliable Pratt and Whitney Twin Wasp engines. The main trick in flying them over long distances, to get the best cruising speed, was to climb above the chosen altitude then put the aircraft into a dive "getting it 'on the step' ," so to speak. Even so, comfortable and good-natured though Liberators were in aerodynamic terms, I never felt that they were natural flying machines. But they added an extra dimension to my experience: I was now qualified to fly single-, twin- and four-engined aircraft and the gateway to India, Karachi, and the routes to it – historic ones in RAF terms – were open to me. My last three months in the Middle East – during which I went back to Bilbeis, this time as an instructor, on Beaufighters – proved to be full, interesting and varied ones in flying terms.

My Liberator conversion course soon "paid off." I got back to Gebel Hamzi on 5 September and on the 6th did an Anson run, to Heliopolis and back; then on the 7th was off with Flt Lt Ken Charlton to India in Liberator KH165. Ken had been on the first course at Kemble; after the war he went into civil aviation, first with Skyways and then with BEA (British European Airways), becoming a Training Captain on BAC One-Elevens. A tall chap with a very confident air, he had a distinctive swagger of the shoulders – which "Red" Williams recognised him by when he saw him again, many years later, at Heathrow. He was a very good, very confident pilot to fly with on my first Liberator run.

This was not only my longest-ever ferry flight (eight hours and 55 minutes from Cairo West to Aden – where we landed at Sheik Othman – and nine hours, 50 minutes from there to Karachi – landing at Mauripur Road): it was without doubt the most spectacular – above some of the most barren landscapes in the world.

From Cairo southwards, over the whole length of Egypt and then the Sudan, we followed the course of the Red Sea – a gleaming blue, far below on our port side.

From Aden, on the 10th, when I was doing the flying, we followed the barren coast of Saudi Arabia, then Muscat and Oman, across the Arabian Sea to Karachi – a nine hours, 50 minutes' flight in an aircraft which provided excellent all-round visibility: its cockpit was high up in the deep-sided fuselage and the high-wing configuration gave an unimpeded downward view. All one had to do was to monitor "George" – the automatic pilot – and keep an eye on the navigation, and monitor the fuel system, especially in transferring fuel from the bomb-bay to the main tanks.

Ken and I spent a couple of nights at Mauripur Road, the main RAF gateway to India, and got ourselves booked on to a Sunderland flight back to Egypt. It left on the 10th, and with a night-stop at Bahrain deposited us the following day at Rod el Farag on the Nile, after a new chapter of experience for me – my first ferry flight in a four-engined aircraft, and by far the longest (approximately 3,200 miles) so far. As was demonstrated in the Battle of the Atlantic, the Consolidated B-24 Liberator was a very-long-range aircraft, which "plugged the gap" in the anti-U-boat campaign. The Liberator Ken Charlton and I had just delivered was to do battle against the Japanese.

In mid-November I did another Liberator trip to India, with Warrant Officers "Paddy" Long and Gould. I've forgotten the latter's nickname; almost everybody had one. Paddy was a soft-spoken Northern Irishman with a gentle sense of humour: one of his *bon mots* I've always remembered was "My memory is what I forget with."

Our timing from Cairo West to Sheik Othman, in Liberator KH124, was slightly better than on my previous trip – 8hr 40min; but on the next leg it was poorer, and because I feared we might be involved in a night landing at Mauripur Road – for which we were not qualified – I decided to land at Masirah Island, off the coast of Muscat & Oman. I don't think the Staging Post personnel there were too pleased to see a big four-engined aircraft lumbering in, but they took it in good part and we left for Karachi the following morning.

It was there the interesting part of this trip began, and what made it unforgettable. Karachi was beset by a combination of the monsoon and high tides; so much so that the buildings comprising the BOAC guest-house were virtually cut off from each other. Nevertheless, Paddy and I decided after dinner that we would go to see a new film, *For Whom the Bell Tolls*. The waiter assured us that we would not get transport – "No sahib, no gharry." Nothing daunted, we set off, and there was a gharry – whose driver promised that he would pick us up after the film.

It was superb – Hemingway's Spanish Civil War story put over unforgettably by Cary Grant and Ingrid Bergman; but it seemed to last for about four hours, and as it was still raining we were dubious about how we were going to get back to the guest-house. But – clip, clop, splash, splash – there was our faithful gharry driver to take us back. I've never forgotten his faithfulness, and hope that his soul rests in peace in some Mohammedan Paradise.

On the 15th we got away on a Dakota flight to Habbaniyah, landing at Bahrain en route; then from there flew to Payne Field, Cairo, in a Curtis Commando of the US Air Transport Command – one of those very big twin-engined aircraft which were used on flights across "the hump" into China.

So it was back to Gebel Hamzi after a second Liberator delivery; but a new surprise awaited me before the end of November – another trip I would never forget, for very different reasons: for on Sunday evening, 22 October, I was startled to learn that I was going to Greece the following day.

The task was to deliver three Spitfires, led by a Baltimore with three Pilot Officers as crew – myself, Charles

Tregoning as navigator and "Willie" Worboys as wireless operator. I couldn't have chosen more acceptable companions: Charles was a Scot with a delightful sense of humour; after the war I met him again when we were planning our first (1947) reunion. He was then working for William Youngers the brewers in London and considerably lubricated our arrangements (but that's another story). "Willie" was a perennially cheerful character; I'm afraid we lost touch with him in the post-war years.

On the 23rd we went across to Cairo West for a special briefing, which was not available, but we got five sets of maps and were told that we would get special "gen"[10] at El Adem. When we got back to Kilo 40 Squadron Leader Dow (A B R Dow, second in command to "Red" Williams, a post Ken Charlton had coveted; he was very put out when he didn't get the promotion) told me that we would have to be back on the following day.

We took off at about 10 o'clock and flew to Helwan (No 132 MU) where the Spitfires were being prepared. After some delay they got airborne; we followed and led them over base in starboard echelon formation, then set course for El Adem. While they proceeded there we landed at Mersa Matruh to drop off a passenger. Our briefing at El Adem was given by a Flight Sergeant who had "been over" to Greece in (I think) a Dakota: it took them two hours and 40 minutes. We reckoned that if we got off by half-past three we would have three hours' daylight.

---

10. i.e. information: "gen" was a term universally used in the wartime RAP.

We did get airborne at about that time, set course for a cape at the start of the Cyrenaica "bulge" in the coastline, and from there to the island of Kythera, flying at 3,000ft in perfect weather. We passed within 24 miles of Crete and could clearly see its highest mountain peak. Just beyond Kythera there was some low cloud over the south-eastern promontory of the Peloponnese, so we put the Spitfires into echelon starboard, but there was no further worry about the weather. We flew just to the east of Piraeus harbour and shortly afterwards, across the bay, could see the widespread city of Athens and Kalamaki aerodrome – which, we discovered, had an awkward hill right on its circuit and another little one at the beginning of a runway; its runways had been bombed but the craters filled in. We landed after two hours 15 minutes' flying time; the Spitfires all got down safely although Tommy Hunter (another Scotsman – from Edinburgh) had to make a flapless landing.

Soon after six o'clock we were driven into Athens in a rickety open truck, along the coastal road. Quite a number of people hitched lifts (there was a noticeable scarcity of transport), others waved to us and we saw quite a profusion of pretty girls. We had a fine view of the Acropolis, standing high up at the end of a long, tree-lined main street.

We went to the Hotel Splendide, which had been taken over by the RAF for transit personnel: the food was bare rations, but conditions were clean and the beds comfortable; the water was off but it came on again in the morning. Dinner consisted of M & V soup, tinned salmon, bully beef and biscuits. Before it we had some beer in a café, at three shillings a bottle. While we were in there everyone rushed out into the street, clapping: a lorryload of troops was passing by.

After dinner we went to the Argentina Cabaret. No one there seemed to get drunk (drinks were very expensive – we bought a bottle of wine for eight shillings), but everyone was tremendously excited. An imitation of Hitler was roared at, *Lili Marlene* sung and danced to (the Allies had entered Athens nine days previously, but there was a real threat of civil war, with the Communist Partisans aiming to take power and the bizarre possibility of British troops being used against them); national dances and songs were wildly applauded. We sat and watched the local scene with fascination for the whole evening, seeing a people for whom the war had ended, who were now free from the domination of their enemy.

Early next morning I went into Jock Craig's room to wake him. He was already awake and said: "Do you want a good view of the Acropolis? – Look out of the window." I opened the shutters: there was the high rock crowned by the Parthenon, under a low, rainy sky; it was a view I shall never forget.

Jock and I, Tommy Hunter and Lomas climbed up to the Parthenon before breakfast; we took several photographs and looked out towards Piraeus and the surrounding cloud-covered hills, over the city's multitudinous little red-tiled houses and its pleasant hilly groves of fir and cypress.

On our way back through the city we stopped at Hadrian's Gate and the perfect fragmentary ruin of the Temple of Zeus to take some more photographs. It was drizzling with rain again as we passed the Government Building, and unfortunately the guards in their picturesque uniforms were inside their sentry boxes. After breakfast (one 'soya link') we went out to Kalamaki aerodrome along the road by the sea.

This time we had three passengers – the three Spitfire pilots – and took off just before 12 o'clock. The weather was sticky up to the Peloponnese, but afterwards perfect. We passed closer to Crete than before and could see it clearly. After a good run from El Adem (an hour and 45 minutes at 10,000ft) we landed at LG237 at 4-40, ending an unforgettable trip.

November 1944 was my last full month at No 2 Ferry Unit (as No 2 ADU had become since the end of September), and with an overlap into early December these final days of Middle East flying proved to be as varied and interesting as their predecessors, with a new dimension added – that of Beaufighter demonstrator.

After the exhilaration of the trip to Athens I found myself trundling the taxi Anson round the Delta area on three successive occasions; then, for three days, flying Wellingtons out of Cairo West. But in five days all was to change: on 11 November I was flown by Anson myself, with Sqn Ldr Young as pilot, to No 1330 Conversion Unit at Bilbeis – this time as an instructor, not a pupil, and that day gave my first demonstration – showing Lt Earle of the South African Air Force how to fly a Beaufighter.

The technique was for the pupil to stand behind the pilot, on the entry/exit hatch, and watch what went on: there were no dual controls. On succeeding days through November I also had Lt Davies and Fg Off Portalis as pupils and demonstrated take-offs and landings, overshoots, stalling, single-engined flying, glide and flapless landings, or with 30° of flap, take-off with 15° of flap and feathering[11] an engine: mastering all these aspects would give them confidence in handling a Beaufighter.

My demonstrator days went on into December, with Sgt Clark as a pupil; but in these last days at Gebel Hamzi – true to form – I also managed to fly a Liberator, a Baltimore, a Spitfire and finally, on 6 December, an Anson, ending those Middle East flying experiences which had begun at Wadi Natrun (LG100) in November 1941 – three years before but a world away in terms of confidence and knowledge, of aircraft and terrain.

I have no recollection at all of my farewell party in the Officers' Mess at RAF Kilo 40/LG237/Gebel Hamzi, except that I remember "Doc" Watson telling me that when I got back to our tent I sat down on my bed and passed out in a state of happy oblivion: we were healthy young fellows, in a benign climate, and could take anything.

Next morning (11 December) Paddy Long and I, tour-expired and posted to the UK, climbed aboard a

---

11. i.e. the propeller stopped, with the blades turned into the slipstream.

Sunderland flying-boat (ML726 – Flt Lt Austin) at Rod el Farag on the Nile in Cairo. We took off for Djerba, an island off the Tunisian coast – an eight hour 15 minutes' flight, leaving behind many memories and crossing that Western Desert territory we had come to know so well. After a night stop (flying-boats offered the most comfortable and leisurely form of air travel) we had a six hour, 45 minutes' flight to Gibraltar, where we were able to do some Christmas shopping. Then on the 13th we flew across a now-liberated France to Plymouth (seven hours, 20 minutes), and after another 40 minutes in our stately Sunderland touched down in Poole harbour for a wartime, Christmastime homecoming after three and a quarter years abroad. In that time, under the impact of a world war, much had changed – as we were soon to discover. But whatever was to happen to us, we possessed indelible memories of our Middle East days, and of those friends with whom we had shared many flying experiences – along the Takoradi route, across the Western Desert, into Tunisia and Algeria, Malta, Cyprus and Greece and out to India, in a variety of aircraft. What were we to do next? After a spot of leave, and reconciliation with our families, we were soon given our marching orders after checking-in with Transport Command HQ at Harrow.

11. Europe 1945

Lincolnshire in winter was a sharp change from the dry, perpetual warmth of Egypt. I had been posted to RAF Coleby Grange, a former fighter station south of Lincoln, now housing No 17 Service Flying Training School. The idea was accustom returned Middle East pilots into the ways and weather of flying in the UK. Things had changed a lot since 1941. The bomber offensive was still going full blast, and in this part of the UK we were surrounded by Lancaster bases.

I had spent Christmas on disembarkation leave with my folks in Manchester – father, mother and sister Margaret in our suburban home in West Didsbury – and reported to Transport Command HQ[12] in Harrow, where I had opted to fly Dakotas. Why I hadn't capitalised on my four-engined flying experience on Liberators, and asked to fly Yorks[13] I don't know; it's easy to be wise after the event. As things turned out, I was in for some pretty varied and valuable flying experience.

---

12. In the Middle East we originally came under MEAF (Middle East Air Force) but were absorbed into Transport Command when it was formed in March 1943.

13. The Avro York, developed from the Lancaster bomber, was a four-engined high-wing transport which entered RAF service for VIP duties in 1943 and for more general duties in 1945. Yorks and Dakotas were the mainstays of the 1945-46 UK-India trooping operation.

No 17 SFTS, which I booked into on a cold, snowy day towards the end of January, was equipped with Airspeed Oxfords – the standard RAF twin-engined trainer. I'd never flown one before, because when I did my SFTS training at Spitalgate (Grantham) in May-July 1941 there was an Anson flight and an Oxford flight (the latter being considered a bit more "tricky" to handle) and I was posted to the former. By now, with a lot of flying experience behind me, the Oxford presented no problems and I liked it as an aircraft. Also the instructors – I remember especially Pilot Officer Beavan and Flying Officer Matthews – were quite relaxed and we got on well together. In the Mess, one character I recall was the Adjutant, Felton Rapley, who was a cinema organist in civilian life.

Flying over the cold Lincolnshire landscape in the winter/spring months of 1945 was like going back to school: the difference was that at SFTS nearly four years earlier I'd been a beginner; now, I had a lot of flying experience behind me – but not in Europe; we were being re-acclimatised, in terms of weather and at night. We did all kinds of exercises in the Oxfords and some in the Link Trainer, that little enclosed box on a three-axial base which enabled all kinds of manoeuvres to be performed without any visual reference: in other words, the pupil pilot had to fly solely by reference to his instruments, as he would have to do at night or in bad weather.

At the end of the course, on 13 March, I received an above-the-average assessment – as I had done when I left No 2 Ferry Unit and also after my stint as a Beaufighter demonstrator. That course at No 17 SFTS had been beneficial and enjoyable, but the nearby Lancaster bases provided a grim reminder of the continuing bomber offensive. One night, when Paddy Long and I were at a theatre in Lincoln, there was a shattering explosion which shook the whole building: no doubt some dreadful accident at Skellingthorpe or Waddington.

Having done my "refresher" on the amiable Oxford (though I might not have thought it so in 1941) I expected to go on a Dakota course, but an interesting interlude was in store – at No 12 Ferry Unit, Melton Mowbray. Not only was I to be involved in more ferrying; I would also fly some new types and find myself in Egypt once again, thanks to the ubiquitous character of Transport Command operations.

After a brief spot of leave (I was flown over to Barton Airport near Manchester – with which I was to become better acquainted after the war – by Flt Sgt Brotherwood on 9 March) I checked-in at Melton Mowbray and on the 15th and 16th was airborne in a Miles Master, the RAF advanced trainer which had a Bristol Mercury engine if it was a Mk III or a Rolls-Royce Kestrel if it was a Mk I – i.e., either a radial or an in-line powerplant. This was an agreeable way of getting my hand in on a single-engine type; it was also an introduction to the Chance-Vought Corsair Naval fighter with a Pratt & Whitney R-2800 radial engine of 2,400 h.p. which I first flew on the 17th and which was to be my mount for my last-ever ferry flight – to Fayid in Egypt (HMS *Phoenix*), which I reached on the

29th after leaving Portreath in Cornwall – the jumping-off point in the UK for overseas reinforcement flights – on the 23rd, an odyssey with one or two complications at its beginning and its ending, perhaps worth relating.

The Corsair was a big, tough fighter – not surprisingly, as it was designed for operations from aircraft carriers – with a distinctive cranked, gull-wing configuration and an unusually high tail-wheel strut. This helped forward visibility when on the ground, giving an almost in-flight attitude and helping the pilot to see past the big radial engine in front of him.

At Portreath some four or five Corsairs formed a convoy, with Rennes in Normandy as a first (refuelling) stop. On take-off from there something delayed me, and by the time I climbed into the sky there was no sign of the other aircraft. But being used to flying on my own, from doing so for three years over the Western Desert and around the Mediterranean, I pressed on to our next scheduled stop – the staging post at Istres on the south coast of France to the west of Marseilles. That was a three hours, 50 minutes flight from Cornwall and I was given night-stop accommodation.

On the 24th I continued my solo journey – to Elmas at the southern end of Sardinia, a staging post with which I was to become very familiar in the autumn/winter months of 1945-46. I was briefed at Istres to fly down the eastern side of Corsica and the western side of Sardinia, instructions which I followed and landed at Elmas – another night stop – after a two hour, 35 minutes flight.

Next day there was another sea crossing – to Castel Benito, Tripoli, with which I was all too familiar – as I was with the rest of my route: four hours, 15 minutes all told from Elmas to Marble Arch, where I night-stopped again. There was some eyebrow-raising along the route that I was flying by myself, but I assured the staging-post personnel of my familiarity with it through long experience.

When I took off from Marble Arch on the 29th for my last leg to Fayid I had to return as I'd forgotten the Form 700 – the aircraft log which is signed by all the fitters and riggers and wireless mechanics to show that all daily checks have been carried out: this delayed me for 15 minutes, then it took me three hours and 40 minutes – with a refuelling stop at El Adem – to make my delivery of Corsair KD187 to HMS *Phoenix* (formerly RAF Fayid) on the shore of the Great Bitter Lake. My reception there, at the end of a long flight, was not too happy – owing to "circumstances beyond my control" (or so I thought).

After landing I had taxied in behind a jeep with Follow Me on his tailboard. Because of the lack of forward visibility behind that big radial engine I had had to zig-zag – inevitably using the brakes; and it was a hot Egyptian afternoon. But when I came to a stop and switched off, I wasn't prepared to be accused by the Engineering Officer (as I suppose he was) of burning-out the brakes. I should have asked him whether he had ever flown a Corsair (which was unlikely), or even taxied one, but in the event – at the end of a long (three hours, 45 minutes) flight – was "caught on the hop" and tongue tied. Often in life one thinks of things one might have said in particular circumstances, but didn't: by then it's too late.

However, I 'phoned No 2 Ferry Unit – as No 2 ADU had become – at Gebel Hamzi (LG237) and the next day they sent an aircraft to collect me – a Miles Martinet, the target-towing aircraft developed from the Miles Master, flown by Fg Off Brooks. This was a 40-minute trip, from the eastern side of Egypt to the base on the Cairo-Alexandria road I knew so well.

It's often said that one should never go back to familiar places, because they will inevitably have changed. When I went into the Mess, three-and-a-half months after leaving it, I felt a stranger. "Red" Williams had left to take command of No 216 Sqn (he'd been succeeded by Wg Cdr H L Dawson); "Adj" Edgell had been posted; there was no sign of "Bud" Abbott – whose Communications Flight had been commended in January for having flown over 6,000 hours without an accident of any kind – nor of "Doc" Watson. However, the Unit was good enough to accommodate me and arrange a passage back to the UK: on 1 April I boarded a BOAC Dakota at Almaza, the Cairo civil airport, for a sedate two-day flight with a night-stop at Castel Benito then to Hum the Bournemouth airfield.

I was still due to do my Dakota conversion, but No 12 Ferry Unit at Melton Mowbray held one or two more surprises. For example, on the 12th I flew a North American P-51 Mustang – probably the finest Allied fighter of the Second World War in terms of range, speed and manoeuvrability: a splendid airframe wrapped around a

Rolls-Royce Packard Merlin powerplant; then on the 15th I flew a Grumman F6F Hellcat Naval fighter. It astonished me, in retrospect, how one just climbed into these different types and flew them, apparently with the utmost confidence. More mundanely, I did passenger-carrying trips in an Oxford and Anson; then on the 20th was myself flown to Leicester East – base of No 1333 Transport Support Conversion Unit.

12. Into the Dakota World

RAF Leicester East was a typical three-runway wartime airfield on the outskirts of the city of Leicester: its role, as the base for No 1333 (Transport Support) Conversion Unit, was to train Dakota crews for squadrons in Nos 46 and 47 Groups of Transport Command. I was there for just over a month, from 20 April to 2 June, a period which overlapped with VE (Victory in Europe) Day, 13 May, when there was a general stand-down. From 26 April, when I had my first flight in a Dakota, until my last sortie in the wartime RAF, on 31 March 1945 in No 46 Sqn, my pilot experience was entirely on this type – the famous and ubiquitous Douglas DC-3/C-47 Dakota, the twin-engined transport which was indispensable to the RAF and USAAF, in Operation Overlord – the Allied landings in Normandy on 6 June 1944 – and the subsequent advance to Berlin.

I'd never flown an aircraft whose cockpit was so high off the ground: entering by the door on the port side, there was quite a steep climb to reach it. Designed in the 1930s (its predecessor the DC-2 had come second in the 1934 London-Melbourne air race), it had a tail-wheel configuration and the two pilots sat about 15ft above the ground, giving them excellent visibility. From there they looked down on the Pratt & Whitney Twin Wasp engines and a generous wing area: the Dakota gave an impression of reliability and safety – fully justified operationally. In the almost 600 hours' flying I subsequently did on the type I never experienced any troubles. Although slow (140kt IAS – indicated air speed) the Dakota was ideally suited to its various transport roles – the carriage of passengers and freight, and paratroop dropping. It had double doors on the port side and its fuselage could be converted according to requirements – with bucket seats along the sides, with more (comparatively) comfortable forward- or rearward-facing seats for longer flights, or completely bare for freight-carrying. I was to experience these conversions for different roles after I joined No 575 Squadron in June 1945, once the No 1333 course – involving day and night handling and cross-countries, paratroop dropping and glider-towing – had been completed by the end of May.

No 575 was one of three Dakota squadrons – the others were Nos 271 and 512 – formed in a new Transport Command Group (No 46) early in 1944 to support Operation Overlord, the Allied invasion of Europe, and they were based on airfields in the Cotswolds: No 575 was at Broadwell and I joined it there in mid-June, but my stay in the Oxfordshire countryside was brief – the squadron had been detached to Brussels (B56-Evere)[14] like Nos 271 and 512.

On the 19th and 20th, doing 7½ hours' flying each day, I was indoctrinated into our ports of call: with Flt Lt Smallwood I visited Y56, B156 and B116 airfields[15], and with Flt Lt Park the same again plus B158, Bl64 and

---

14. All the "invasion airfields" were numbered.
15. i.e. Munchengladbach, Luneburg, and Wunsdorf.

BI60[16]. Then for three days which I will never forget I took part in the repatriation of Russian DPs (displaced persons) from Munchen-Gladbach to Luneburg, from where they were transported back to the Soviet Union, to whatever fate Stalin had in store for them.

In that summer of 1945, only a month after the German surrender and Allied victory, Europe bore the scars of war with ruined cities and the countryside pock-marked with bomb craters. The thousands of people the Nazis had forcibly imported as slave labour in their armament factories were to be sent home: the queues of Dakotas filled up with men and women clutching their small possessions. I remember one particularly attractive, lively Russian girl who came up into the cockpit; she was clearly delighted with the prospect of getting back to her native land after the grim wartime years in Germany, but I wonder what befell her and the other DPs when they got back to the Soviet Union: probably a merciless, gruesome retribution for having fallen into enemy hands.

In the month I spent at Brussels-Evere (the city was in sight from the airfield and one of the No 512 Sqn pilots had got himself fixed up with a wealthy Belgian mistress with a convenient apartment) I came to realise two things: that the skies of Western Europe were now clear and safe and peaceful, after five years and eight months when they had been the ceaseless domain of fighter and bomber aircraft; and that the ubiquitous and reliable Dakota could

---

16. i.e Lubeck, Schleswigland and Kastrup.

be used to carry passengers and freight whenever and wherever required. On 30 June we positioned at Croydon to carry the WAAF Band to The Hague: unfortunately the weather was poor and they had a rough ride; but I remember that they soon recovered their musicianly spirits when they got to their destination and went on parade.

Four days earlier we had been to Stavanger, Norway, which I was to visit again in post-war years; and at the beginning of July one day's operations encompassed four European capitals – Oslo, Copenhagen, Paris (Le Bourget) and Brussels. On a beautiful summery afternoon we were returning from Berlin (Gatow) to Brussels under a calm, windless sky with "George" the automatic pilot doing the flying when I felt an urgent tap on my right shoulder and heard a voice which said urgently "Brussels" – emphasised by a finger pointing downwards through the front windscreen. Fortunately, our wiry wireless operator had stayed awake: I had nodded off under the somnolent conditions; to my right was a sleeping co-pilot and behind me the navigator was out for the count with his head on the plotting-table; so, good for our New Zealand W/Op, otherwise we might have found ourselves cruising over the North Sea.

Of less innocuous memory was a trip we made from Brussels to Le Bourget on 10 July, with 26 French DPs aboard. One of those poor fellows, who had survived forced labour in the German armament factories, had a gangrenous leg and the stench in the passenger cabin was awful: fortunately the flight was only an hour and a quarter long.

My month on the Brussels detachment was coming to an end and by mid July I was back at Broadwell: on the 16th I did a trip to Berlin with a new crew and on the 21st went to Edzell on the east coast of Scotland, bringing down a couple of WAAF officers to Leicester East (shades of No 1333 TSCU, which already felt like a long time ago); and finally on 27 July I flew up to Melbourne near York, where a former bomber squadron, No 10, had been transferred from Bomber to Transport Command and later that year, re-equipped with Dakotas, was re-located to India. No doubt KN296, which I took there, was one of these. This was my last flight on No 575 Sqn, which had afforded me some bird's-eye views of Europe in the immediate aftermath of five years and eight months of total war: I was grateful for the experience, but humbled by it. No sooner had I got to Melbourne than I was flown to Ringway, Manchester, by Fg Off Calderwood in an Oxford to go on leave before my next posting – again to a Dakota squadron, No 525, which had a long-range trooping role in No 47 Group of Transport Command. This meant flying UK-India and back through the autumn-winter-spring of 1945-46. That, as they say, is another story: for a few weeks I could enjoy some suburban home comforts.

13. Passages to India – and back

Before the end of 1944 the British Chiefs of Staff approved a policy of large-scale air trooping, to come into effect after the defeat of Germany. This was to support Operation Dracula, a seaborne and airborne attack on Rangoon proposed by Admiral Lord Louis Mountbatten. The aim of this was to drive the Japanese out of Burma. With the war in Europe estimated to end by 30 June 1945, it was intended that large-scale air trooping would begin in July.

The dropping of atomic bombs on Hiroshima and Nagasaki on 6 and 9 August and the subsequent Japanese surrender eliminated the prospect of a Far East offensive, but the plan for large-scale air trooping was retained, with a change of purpose – to bring home as many Servicemen as possible, with the aim of revitalising the UK economy. Inevitably, because the India-Burma theatre was being denuded of personnel through repatriation, replacements were required: so the Yorks, Dakotas, Liberators, Halifaxes and Stirlings which went back and forth between the UK and Karachi like an airborne conveyor belt were fully loaded both ways; and the whole Trooping Programme – Reinforcement and Repatriation[17] – was a major exercise in

---

17. The title given to the chapter on the Trooping Programme in *Forged in War: A History of Royal Air Force Transport Command* 1943-1967 by Humphrey Wynn (HMSO, 1996).

logistics, with Staging Posts strung out along the route catering for the servicing of both aircraft and personnel.

Because RAF Transport Command itself could not cope with the number of aircraft required from its own resources of Yorks, Dakotas and Liberators, aircraft from Bomber and Coastal Commands were drafted into service as transports[18].

As a very small cog in this very large transport wheel, after my leave I reported to my new squadron – No 525, based at RAF Membury, a wartime airfield in the Berkshire Downs, near Lambourn, famous for its racing stables. I began flying there on 25 August with a half-hour dual check under the watchful eye of Flt Lt Miles; then with a crew – Fg Off Alleston and Warrant Officers Bibey and Carnochan – did an hour and a half self-motivated check which included single-engine flying and a flapless landing. Then on the 26th we did a cross-country – up to Rhyl in North Wales, along the coast to Blackpool, then down to Manchester – my home town, where with a slight diversion we managed to fly over the suburb of West Didsbury where I was born and saw my mother waving to us in the garden – for a few minutes I occupied that piece of sky I had looked up into so often in my boyhood days – and back to base. The weather was perfect, but as we approached Manchester from the Lancashire coast I noticed that it had its own local

---

18. In *Winged Life* A Biography of David Beaty MBE DFC (Airlife Publishing, 2001) Betty Campbell Beaty describes how his Coastal Command Liberator squadron, No 206, was converted for troop carrying with the armament taken out, eight seats put into the bomb bay and 18 in the fuselage.

climate – a misty aura, no doubt occasioned by dampness in the atmosphere, the historic reason for the city's success in the cotton trade.

I got to know Pete Carnochan well and once asked him what he was going to do after demobilisation. "Go back to my old job, I expect," he said. "What's that?" I asked. "Making suits for dead people," he explained – a euphemism for his work in the undertaking department of the Co-op in Leeds. I hope things went well for him; there would never be any shortage of business.

Later that day I was given a night-flying check by Flt Lt Mullin; then, with Pete as wireless operator, did four night flying circuits.

I had been accepted into my new squadron and a week later, on 2 September, was ready to set off for India on my first trooping run.

We were instructed to position at Merryfield, a West Country airfield near Taunton, and flew in there on 2 September. Great was my pleasure at bumping into Frank Fenn when I walked into the Mess that evening. I'd known him well in the Middle East; he was now on No 187 Sqn, one of the other Dakota squadrons on the trooping programme. He was serving in the Metropolitan Police when policemen were allowed to volunteer for the RAF and went back to the Met after the war, doing very well and becoming a Chief Superintendent. I had a high regard for Frank and was delighted to see him again.

I was also lucky in having Ray Groves – "Kitty" Groves as he was called on No 2 ADU – as my co-pilot: we were to fly over much of the terrain that was familiar to us from Middle East days, and I couldn't have had a more equable and cheerful companion.

The Dakotas were the slowest and shortest-range aircraft on the trooping programme: they had to make more refuelling stops than the four-engined types, nine as against five for the Yorks. The longest stage for a Dakota was 880 nautical miles in a scheduled flying time of seven hours, while a York could cover 1,300 n.m. in seven-and-a-half hours. What it was going to be like in practice we were soon to discover.

The principle on which Transport Command operated the programme was that of slip crews. An aircraft flew its required stage length, then the crew handed it over and had a night stop; they then took on another aircraft at whatever time of the day or night it came in. I used to make sure that the crew compartment was left in a tidy condition, with all controls set at neutral. The Service passengers had about two hours on the ground, with a meal, then were taken on by the slip crew. I always felt sorry for them; it must have been a slow and excruciatingly boring mode of travel, but being Servicemen they didn't – or couldn't – complain.

With Ray Groves, Warrant Officer Bibey and Flt Lt Powell I took off on the 3rd from Merryfield with a full load (24 passengers) bound for Elmas at the southern end of Sardinia, our first stop: it took us six hours, 50 minutes and we found ourselves in a warm, sunny, dry climate; during the winter months this was a perfect antidote to coughs and colds contracted in the UK – they disappeared in no time.

On the 4ᵗʰ we left by night for El Adem, so what should have been a shimmering blue Mediterranean far below was darkness and void for the five hours and 50 minutes to a Western Desert staging post I had known so well over the last three years – though I'd never before landed there at night. Once more we were accommodated – one recalls with gratitude the staging post personnel who refuelled and serviced the aircraft and provided the crews with meals and beds – and on the 5ᵗʰ took off on a four-hour flight to Lydda in Palestine (as it was then – still under the British Mandate).

In that 1945-46 era, Palestine was a quiet and well-governed country, with a wonderfully invigorating climate: we used to buy oranges and grapefruit there, in large round baskets, to take home to fruit-starved Britain. Palestinians served in the RAF and – although the seeds of Israeli nationalism, to be nurtured shortly by the Stern Gang and Irgun Zvei Leumi with their atrocities against British Service personnel, and before the Jewish immigrations from Europe – there was a façade of order and good Government and we were untroubled in our transit stops at Lydda.

On one occasion when we staged through Lydda, Ray Groves and I went down to the River Jordan to collect some water for the christening of his nephew. I remember that we took a taxi from Jerusalem, and the New Testament phrase "went down from Jerusalem to Jericho" came to life for us: Jerusalem is 2,300 ft above sea level, Jericho is 1,292ft below it – a descent of nearly 4,000ft in ten miles.

One of the sharers of our taxi was a handsome Arab in his kefiyeh who could have come straight from the pages of T.E. Lawrence's *Seven Pillars of Wisdom* – an aristocratic personage with innate dignity.

Ray collected some of the rather muddy water of the Jordan in a small bottle he had brought with him and took it back on one of our return flights to the UK (he was my co-pilot on three of my six trooping flights to Karachi).

On the 7th we took off for Habbaniyah, that famous old RAF station in the Iraqi desert, some 60 miles west of Baghdad. I'd last seen it in 1942 when I contracted malaria when en route for China in that P-40E convoy, so it didn't hold a very happy memory for me; but this time we staged through without incident and took our troops on to Bahrain.

This flight – climbing out from Lydda across the bare Judean hills and mountains of Moab which border Palestine to the east – had associations with the 1920s when the RAF was given responsibility for air control over Iraq, for its Vimys and Victorias heading for Hinaidi followed this same route – the oil pipeline from Basrah to Haifa, across inhospitable desert, with an oasis when the great Habbaniyah base was completed in 1937.

When we landed at Bahrain by night on the 7th and expected to proceed from there when the next aircraft came in, we were in for a surprise; for on the 8th a Dakota of No 216 Sqn (a bomber/transport squadron which had been in the Middle East since after the First World War) took us to Shaibah, near Basrah at the head of the Persian Gulf, a station which in song and legend had the reputation of being the most unpopular posting in the RAF.

We were not there long enough to contract "those Shaibah Blues" as the song has it (endured by personnel posted there for two or three years): on the 12th we resumed our flight to Karachi and this time there were no glitches. By night to Bahrain took an hour and 55 minutes; then a much longer leg to Mauripur Road, our Karachi destination, which took six hours, 35 minutes into rising daylight – something which never failed to thrill me as we flew eastwards: I thought of those familiar lines from the hymn, "as o'er each continent and island the dawn leads on another day."

This was a part of the world I hadn't seen before – a barren landscape indeed. Overflying Sharjah, where my P-40E flight had ended in 1942, we saw far below the narrow neck of the Gulf of Oman which guards the entrance to the Persian Gulf; then, for endless miles, the dry rugged coastline of Iran, then the barren vista of Baluchistan – which became part of West Pakistan after Partition in 1947 – and finally the then gateway to India, Karachi, where we landed on the 12th – a small pawn in the gigantic logistical chess game known as the Air Trooping Programme, master-minded by Transport Command, its Groups and en route Staging Posts, like so many stations on an inter-continental railway system.

With the constant build-up of aircraft and transit personnel there, Mauripur's main concern was to get rid of both as quickly as possible: on the following day (13

September) we were sent off westwards in the same aircraft, KN238, and again had a disjointed journey – six and a quarter hours to Bahrain, then on the following day two hours, 35 minutes to Shaibah.

We must by then have been a spare crew, because we completed the rest of our journey back to the UK as passengers – in Dakotas of No 216 Sqn, which took us to Habbaniyah, then from there via Lydda to Almaza, Cairo; then in a Short Stirling from Cairo West to Castel Benito (five hours, 20 minutes) and from there to Lyneham (seven hours, 50 minutes), which we reached on 20 September and were lifted from by Dakota to Membury – one of our own squadron aircraft flown by Flt Lt Miles: we'd been away from base for 18 days.

I never forgot my one and only ride in a Stirling, that huge Shorts bomber which suffered operationally by comparison with the more successful Avro Lancaster and Handley Page Halifax, which it preceded into Bomber Command service. Stirlings were used on the Large-scale Trooping Operation (as it was called), and we were flown back from Cairo West by Flg Off Oakeby, a New Zealander. I asked him jokingly whether they ever bounced on landing; for with the cockpit so high off the ground, getting back on to it must have taken some judging, though no doubt the pilots got used to it. I had to eat my words when we landed at Lyneham: I was sitting right in the rear of the aircraft, and the tail-wheel oleo leg (which I understand there were some initial problems with, so that it had to be re-designed) hit the ground with such a bang that

I thought it would come up through the fuselage: maybe it always sounded like that. Anyway, we were back safely in the UK and were sent on a week's leave. There was no "station" life at Membury (where I encountered WAAFs for the first time): our way of life for the next five months, until early March 1946, became a regular routine – a trooping run to India and back, then leave, then off again along the route. It was a theme with variations – some of them interesting and unexpected. Underlying it was the reliability of our aircraft: I was never let down by the Dakota in all those long hours of day and night flying (82 hours 35 minutes in the peak month of October 1945 when Large Scale Trooping was initiated and 76 hours five minutes in the following month; thereafter averaging over 60 hours a month).

The Dakotas were the slowest and the lowest-flying (we used to cruise at 8-10,000ft) aircraft on the trooping run, so the weather across France and over the Mediterranean – where there could be some pretty nasty storms – was always a problem. We used the "Carcassone gap" between the Pyrenees and the Massif Central, where we were clear of the mountains, when the weather was really bad across France; over the Mediterranean, we had to take it as it came: I was always sorry for our soldier passengers when it was really rough – though when UK-bound I don't suppose they really cared; they were being repatriated after three or four years in the Far East.

On 3 October we positioned at Brussels (Melsbroek) where we embarked our Army passengers for their long, slow flight to Karachi. I still had my amicable crew – Ray Groves, Warrant Officer Bibey as navigator, and the ever-cheerful Pete Carnochan – and from there to Elmas took four hours, 40 minutes. I always enjoyed my brief visits to Sardinia: the climate was warm and equitable; there was much to see locally – especially the troglodytes, the cave-dwellers in the rocky cliffs to the north of Cagiliari; and on one occasion we had the inestimable pleasure of hearing Benjiamino Gigli sing in an open-air opera performance. Troubled by a fly which persistently attempted to land on his nose, Gigli provided facial expressions above and beyond those demanded by the music he was performing.

We went on via El Adem on the 3rd/4th to Cairo West (two hours, 50 minutes by day and two hours, 40 minutes by night) and when we made our approach on the glide slope indicator – showing a yellow if you were too high, a red if you were too low and a green if you were right – I had my only glitch with Ray Groves in all our flying together: I yelled at him to put down full flap, but he had already selected full flap – I was too high and we were going to overshoot, which I did by applying full power. So we "went round again," and the next time I got it right. I have often wondered what our passengers thought about what was going on "up front;" but perhaps – happily – they thought everything was quite normal.

On the 5th we left in the same aircraft (KN492) for Habbaniyah, with an ATS Sergeant as passenger (I suppose she was on posting and we were the next available aircraft); and from there to Mauripur Road our destinations and loads – not soldiers on the trooping run – were somewhat quixotic: freight to Bahrain, then vegetables to Jask on the coast of Iran, where I hope they were welcomed.

I described this conclusion of a trooping flight in a previously mentioned book[19] which recorded that among the arrivals at Mauripur during October was Dakota KN416 of No 525 Sqn which came in on the 7th; that we had "picked it up at Habbaniyah under the 'shuttle' system whereby aircraft were taken on while the incoming crew rested at a staging post." I recalled that it had been "flown with a load of freight to Bahrain, and of vegetables from there to Jask; from Mauripur it went on to Poona [a four-hour, five minutes flight], returning on same day."

We left Karachi on the late evening of the 9th for our return to the UK – after an interminable delay, with crew and passengers on board, when the lights grew dimmer and dimmer as the internal power supply was used up – by an alternative route, the "long way round," via Aden and Wadi Haifa.

This was a long haul for a slow aircraft – three hours, 40 minutes to Masirah Island (where, in October 1944, I had previously landed in a Liberator) and six hours, ten minutes in the darkness along the invisible barren landscape of Muscat & Oman and Southern Arabia to Aden. Then another six-and-a-half-hour stage – five hours by night and an hour-and-a-half in daylight to Wadi Haifa on the Nile, which I'd last landed at in a Hurricane on 14 August 1942,

---

19. *Forged in War: A History of Royal Air Force Transport Command 1943-1967* (HMSO, 1966).

on my last convoy flight up the West African Reinforcement Route – ancient history, as far as the air aspect of the Second World War was concerned: the Desert War and Operation Overlord were now things of the past – we were bringing home veterans of the Far East War.

This time, however, we flew not up the Nile to Cairo but bearing north-eastwards to Lydda, Palestine (as always, a welcome source of oranges and grapefruit to take home to fruit starved Britain, and an agreeable night-stop in that beautiful climate); then four hours and ten minutes to El Adem, half of it by day and half by night, and five hours, 55 minutes to Elmas, Sardinia – for us, another night-stop. Finally, on 15 October, a home run (five hours, 50 minutes) to Membury. At the end of that month Air Marshal Sir Ralph Cochrane, AOC-in-C Transport Command, sent out a signal: "Please pass to all ranks engaged in the Large Scale Trooping programme my personal congratulations on the success achieved during the first month of operations. Target figures in both directions were exceeded .... " So at least our long flights to and from India, and those people on the ground who supported them, were appreciated.

14. Into the New Forest and out of the RAF

During January 1946, in the large-scale trooping programme, 2,809 troops were flown back to the UK and 2,766 flown out; and on the 12th the two Dakota bases, Membury and Broadwell, were notified that the UK-India and return trooping rate was to be reduced: the programme was being wound down.

In January I made my fifth trooping run, and in February-March my sixth and last, with some changes in my crew: Ray Groves had been demobbed; I had Fg Off Hunt and then WO Fenton as co-pilot, Flt Lt House – with a soft-spoken Dorset accent, who hailed from Blandford Forum – as navigator, and the ever-faithful, cheerful WO Pete Carnochan as wireless operator. Throughout my time on No 525 Sqn I couldn't have wished for better crew members; we worked amicably as a team. Happily, we were posted as a crew when the trooping programme ended – to No 46 Sqn at Stoney Cross in the New Forest.

On our last "home run" I had a slight contretemps when taxying at Lydda, when the tailplane of KN241 struck an oil drum used as a marker (I was following the airman's signals, as I thought, but there seemed to be some misunderstanding): repairs were effected and on 28

February I air-tested the aircraft; then on 1 March we were off again, with 19 passengers – diverted to Cairo West.

This last trooping run was a slightly chequered one – to the very end, for on the 5th we returned to Lydda, then set off for the UK via El Adem, Castel Benito, then Istres (west of Marseilles) – from where we were diverted to Lyneham because of fog at Membury: when it cleared we did the 15-minute hop to Membury, on 8 March. I had flown 390 hours, 25 minutes on No 525 Sqn and extended my knowledge of world geography eastwards to India. The squadron had played its part in the huge and successful UK-India trooping programme. There was to be a brief coda to my RAF flying experience.

In mid-March my crew and I were posted to No 46 Sqn at Stoney Cross, an airfield in the New Forest, just north of the A31 road to Ringwood and Bournemouth and not far from the Rufus Stone where William Rufus, eldest son of William the Conqueror, was killed by an arrow in 1100 when out hunting. The airfield was one of those built in 1944 to house Allied Air Forces' squadrons for the invasion of Europe, Operation Overlord: US IXth Air Force P-38 Lightning and B-26 Maurauder squadrons were based there.

In the spring of 1946, however, lovely though the area was with the grass and scent of gorse in warm sunshine, the station was in a kind of time warp: there seemed to be a general indifference, a lack of enthusiasm now that the war was over and most people were waiting to be demobbed. Even our squadron number was unreal, for No 46 Sqn had

Hurricanes in 1940 and took part in the ill-fated Norwegian campaign;[20] it had nearly always been a fighter squadron but latterly had operated Stirlings in the transport role before being re-equipped with Dakotas. Nevertheless, I was proud to have been on it, if only for a few days – from the 25th to the end of March, in flying terms.

I started off doing some night-flying circuits and landings with Pilot Officers Sewell and Goulding, then with my crew (WO Fenton, Flt Lt House and Pete Carnochan) did a couple of days of air tests and exercises (Gee approaches, QGH, BABS and single-engined landings), then on the 29th air-tested Dakota KN408 – the last aircraft I was to fly in the wartime RAF – to prepare it for a scheduled service to Gibraltar.

We took off on the 30th for Istres with 11 passengers, but were delayed when we got there because of an unserviceability, so it was night when we landed at the famous Rock – such a crucial base during the war years. On the 31st we returned, again via Istres, with 15 passengers; and when we touched down at Stoney Cross I realised it was just over five years since I'd started to fly at No 16 EFTS (Elementary Flying Training School) at Burnaston, Derby. I'd now done 1924hr 25 minutes as a pilot in 22 different types of aircraft – productive flying, even though

---

20. Its Hurricanes were lost, together with those of No 263 Sqn and all their personnel except for two pilots, when HMS *Glorious* was sunk in the evacuation from Norway, after having been successfully "landed on": see *Straight and Level*, the autobiography of Air Chief Marshal Sir Kenneth Cross (Grub Street, 1993).

not heroic or dangerous – and had come to know the African/Middle East parts of the world. I had also made many enduring friendships; for it is in such circumstances one comes to know one's fellow men – without any prejudices of politics or religion or social status – for what they really are. For all such rich wartime experiences, in the air and on the ground, I was profoundly grateful to the RAF.

Epilogue

The RAF gave me many friendships – made under circumstances when one didn't know anything about a chap's background – his social status, politics or religion: one liked him for what he was. These friendships have endured, through meetings, letters and reunions. The first No 2 Aircraft Delivery Unit reunion was held at the Connaught Rooms, London, on 27 September 1947 and the 50th in the Officers' Mess, RAF Duxford, on 17 September 1997 – fifty years to the day after the first.

I am inexpressibly grateful to the RAF for the friendships I have made, and for the wartime flying experiences I had – everything dating from that day in September 1939 when I crossed Oxford Road, Manchester, from the University to the Recruiting Office to volunteer my services to the RAF.

The explanation of my title is that, in six years' continuous flying in the wartime RAF, I never fired a gun in anger or dropped any bombs or depth-charges.

H.W. 2008

Index